A HOUSE DIVIDED

Meech Lake, Senate Reform and the Canadian Union

D1189463

A HOUSE DIVIDED

Meech Lake, Senate
Reform and the Canadian Union

by

Gordon Robertson

The Institute for Research on Public Policy
L'Institut de recherches politiques

Printed in Canada

Legal Deposit Fourth Quarter
Bibliothèque nationale du Québec

Canadian Cataloguing in Publication Data

Robertson, Gordon, 1917-

A house divided

Prefatory material in English and French.
Includes bibliographical references.
ISBN 0-88645-096-9

1. Federal government—Canada.   2. Federal-
provincial relations—Canada. *
3. Canada. Constitution Act, 1982.
4. Canada—Constitutional law—Amendments.
5. Canada. Parliament. Senate.—Reform.
I. Institute for Research on Public Policy.
II. Title.

JL27.R62 1989   321.02'0971   C89-098673-8

Camera-ready copy and publication management by
PDS Research Publishing Services Limited
P.O. Box 3296
Halifax, Nova Scotia B3J 3H7

Published by The Institute for Research on Public Policy
L'Institut de recherches politiques
P.O. Box 3670 South
Halifax, Nova Scotia B3J 3K6

*And if a house be divided against itself,
that house cannot stand.*

The Gospel according to St. Mark
Chapter 3, Verse 25

Table of Contents

A HOUSE DIVIDED

Foreword

In the 100 years following creation of its federal structure in 1867, Canada became one of the most successful and prosperous countries in the world. But that successful federation rested on an unequal balance between the two founding linguistic groups. In the 1950s and 1960s, a new generation in Quebec demanded the scope within Confederation for a fully modern, dynamic, and enduring society operating in French. Canadians have spent the last 20 years trying to establish new terms for the union of 1867 to meet this new situation.

That search led from the work of the "B & B Commission", reporting in 1967, through the launching of the constitutional review in 1968, the Quebec referendum of 1980, "patriation" of the Constitution in 1982, to the Quebec proposals of 1986, and appeared to reach its goal with the Meech Lake Accord of 1987.

But it is apparent that, after a strong start in 1987 and 1988, the Meech Lake Accord is now in difficulty. It has not yet received the approval of two provinces—Manitoba and New Brunswick—and that approval now looks anything but sure. The new government in Newfoundland has hinted at the possibility of withdrawing the approval given by its legislature before the last election. All governments have, so far at least, operated on the basis that the

Accord will die if it does not have the unanimous approval of the provinces by June, 1990.

While it is in Manitoba that formal approval is lacking so far as the West is concerned, the difficulties there reflect a growing resistance to the Accord in all four Western provinces. The sources of western concern are various, but in part they arise from a sense of frustration about seemingly endless attention to a Quebec problem with no attention to what the West feels to be equally valid western problems about our federal structure.

In New Brunswick and Newfoundland some of the sources of concern about the Accord appear to be different from those in the West but others have a familiar ring to western ears. In any case, it is clear that both in the Atlantic provinces and in the West some way must be found to alleviate regional concerns if support for the Meech Lake Accord is to revive.

Is the approval of the Accord important? Despite criticisms of some provisions within it, it would be rash to believe that the Accord can be lost without serious risks. There is unlikely to be any better means, or any better chance, to resolve the present impasse. No one has proposed any alternative basis, acceptable to all 11 governments and legislatures in Canada, for achieving the willing acceptance by Quebec of the 1982 constitutional amendments to which it did not agree.

The very fact that the Meech Lake Accord was negotiated and accepted by 11 governments, and that it has been approved by nine elected legislatures, has created a new situation. If the Accord collapses, Canada would not simply revert to the situation pre-Meech Lake. The loss of the dynamic toward an agreed constitution, and the rejection of an initiative for agreement by a federalist government in Quebec, could have consequences far more serious than whatever difficulties there may be in specific provisions of the Accord itself. We could have the worst of all worlds: no agreed constitution and no way to tackle the changes people want made.

It is to this complex of problems that Gordon Robertson addresses himself in this short book. It is his belief that the concerns of the West and of the Atlantic provinces must be taken seriously and that effective Senate reform would be the most convincing measure to address some of them. He argues that there is not a 1990 deadline on

FOREWORD

approval of the Meech Lake Accord so there is time to take on Senate reform without losing the Accord. If both Accord and Senate reform were proceeding together, there might be a lessening of frustrations that would permit both Quebec and the Western and Atlantic provinces to feel that a more acceptable balance had been achieved in our federal system. Agreement on both might prove possible, and might thus lead the way to some of the further changes advocated with respect to women's rights, the position of the Northern territories, or the constitutional expression of aboriginal rights.

Canada's first 120 years of Confederation have been a great success story. We have shown during these years a remarkable capacity to achieve accommodations among widely differing peoples and regions. The success of our next 100 years may depend on whether we succeed or fail in achieving agreement on the constitutional issues that are now before us. Mr. Robertson's proposals, made after 20 years of work on federal-provincial relations and constitutional questions, may help in the discussions of governments and the debates among Canadians in the months ahead.

Rod Dobell
President
September 1989

Avant-propos

Les cent ans qui ont suivi la création de la structure fédérale du Canada en 1867 ont vu ce pays réussir et devenir l'un des plus prospères au monde. Malheureusement, le succès de cette fédération repose sur un équilibre précaire entre ses deux groupes linguistiques fondateurs. Dans les années 1950 et 1960, la nouvelle génération de Québécois demandait pour le Québec une place dans la confédération en tant que société moderne, dynamique et durable fonctionnant en français. Les Canadiens ont passé les 20 dernières années à essayer d'établir de nouvelles formules qui permettraient à l'union de 1867 de s'adapter à cette nouvelle situation.

Cette recherche a fait son chemin, avec la "Commission B & B" et son rapport en 1967, le lancement de la révision constitutionnelle en 1968, le référendum du Québec de 1980, le "rapatriement" de la Constitution en 1982 et les propositions du Québec de 1986; le but semblait presque atteint avec l'Accord du lac Meech en 1987.

Il est toutefois devenu apparent que, après un bon départ en 1987 et 1988, l'Accord du lac Meech se trouve en difficulté. Il n'a pas encore reçu l'approbation de deux provinces, le Manitoba et le Nouveau-Brunswick, et cette approbation semble aujourd'hui compromise. Le nouveau gouvernement de Terre-Neuve a fait savoir qu'il envisageait de retirer l'accord donné par son assemblée législative avant les dernières élections. Jusqu'ici, les gouvernements ont agi en partant du principe que l'Accord deviendrait caduc s'il ne recevait pas l'approbation unanime des provinces d'ici juin 1990.

Bien que le Manitoba soit la seule province de l'Ouest qui n'ait pas encore donné son approbation officielle, les difficultés rencontrées dans cette région reflètent la résistance grandissante des quatre provinces de l'Ouest envers l'Accord. Les origines de ces préoccupations sont nombreuses; elles proviennent cependant en partie de la frustration éprouvée devant le fait que l'attention générale semble se porter indéfiniment sur les problèmes du Québec au détriment de l'Ouest et de ses problèmes, que celui-ci considère comme étant aussi importants en ce qui concerne notre structure fédérale.

Au Nouveau-Brunswick et à Terre-Neuve, certaines des réserves vis-à-vis de l'Accord semblent avoir des origines différentes, alors que d'autres ressemblent fort à celles de l'Ouest. En tout état de cause, il est clair que, dans les provinces de l'Atlantique aussi bien que dans l'Ouest, il faudra trouver un moyen d'apaiser les préoccupations actuelles si l'on veut faire revivre le soutien de l'Accord du lac Meech.

Est-il donc tellement important que cet Accord soit approuvé? En dépit des critiques formulées à l'égard de certaines de ses clauses, il serait certes téméraire de penser que l'Accord puisse être abandonné sans aucun risque. Il ne semble pas que l'on puisse trouver un meilleur moyen, ou une meilleure occasion, de débloquer l'impasse où nous nous trouvons à l'heure actuelle. Personne n'a encore proposé de solution de rechange susceptible d'être acceptée par les onze gouvernements et assemblées législatives du Canada, et qui permette d'amener le Québec à donner volontairement son assentiment aux amendements constitutionnels de 1982, avec lesquels il n'est pas d'accord.

Le fait même que l'Accord du lac Meech ait été négocié et accepté par onze gouvernements, et qu'il ait été approuvé par neuf assemblées législatives élues, crée une nouvelle situation. Si l'Accord n'est pas ratifié, le Canada ne sera plus en mesure de reprendre les choses là où elles en étaient restées avant l'épisode du lac Meech. La perte du dynamisme visant à l'instauration d'une constitution acceptée par tous et le rejet d'un accord préparé à l'initiative d'un gouvernement fédéraliste au Québec pourraient avoir des conséquences bien plus dommageables que l'importance réelle des difficultés que peuvent

AVANT-PROPOS

susciter certaines clauses de l'Accord lui-même. Nous pourrions nous retrouver dans le pire des mondes possibles: pas d'accord sur la constitution et aucun moyen d'effectuer les changements que tout le monde réclame.

C'est ce problème épineux que Gordon Robertson examine dans ce court volume. Il est d'avis que les préoccupations de l'Ouest et des provinces de l'Atlantique doivent être prises au sérieux et qu'une bonne réforme du sénat serait le moyen le plus approprié de répondre à certaines d'entre elles. Selon lui, la date limite de 1990 pour l'approbation de l'Accord du lac Meech n'a pas lieu d'exister, ce qui fait qu'il serait tout à fait possible de procéder à une réforme du sénat sans pour cela négliger l'avenir de l'Accord. Si les deux réformes, celle de l'Accord et celle du sénat, étaient entreprises en même temps, les frustrations de part et d'autre s'en verraient quelque peu apaisées, et le Québec et les provinces de l'Ouest et de l'Atlantique pourraient avoir l'impression que l'on est parvenu à un meilleur équilibre dans notre système fédéral. Il est dans le domaine du possible que ces deux réformes s'avèrent acceptables et ouvrent la voie à d'autres changements préconisés relativement aux droits de la femme, à la situation des territoires du Nord ou à l'expression constitutionnelle des droits des autochtones.

Les 120 premières années du Canada en tant que confédération ont été une grande réussite. Au cours de ces années, nous avons prouvé d'une façon remarquable que nous pouvions arriver à des compromis, malgré la diversité de nos populations et de nos régions. La réussite des cent prochaines années risque de dépendre du succès ou de l'échec de la résolution des questions actuelles relatives à la constitution. Les propositions de M. Robertson, qui sont l'aboutissement de 20 ans de travail dans le domaine des relations fédérales-provinciales et des questions constitutionnelles, pourront peut-être faciliter les discussions des gouvernements et les débats entre les Canadiens au cours des mois à venir.

Rod Dobell
Président
Septembre 1989

Preface

In early 1988 I was invited to participate in the Annual Conference of the Institute of Public Administration of Canada to be held the following September. It was to be on the theme of the challenges posed for Canada in the years ahead "by the imperative of world competition". I was asked to talk about how our federal system might be adapted to face those challenges. After some remarks about the necessity of federalism for a country of regions and divisions such as Canada, I said that, if one were designing a system of government for maximum efficiency to meet external competitive challenges—or even many of the internal challenges of government—one would not choose a federal system at all. However, Canada could not exist without one. There is too much regional and cultural difference for people to be prepared to entrust everything to one central government. The question was what to do—or what not to do—that would make us best able to survive and, if possible, to thrive in an increasingly competitive world with steadily more complex problems both at home and abroad.

I suggested that one thing we should do was whatever minimum was really essential to put our federal structure in good order, and then escape from the constitutional wrangles that had absorbed so much of the attention, energy and time of our governments, leaders and people in the last 20 years.

I said I thought there were two major deficiencies in our federalism that did have to be addressed because, without resolution of them, Canada would not have the essential acceptance of our political structure that would permit the country to operate without the conflicts that so often divert us from the substance of policies and confuse our national purpose. One of the major problems was the unacceptability to Quebec of the Constitution as revised, without its agreement, in 1982. I said that "if we are to avoid things that could diminish Canada's capacity to meet the challenge of world competition in the future, I can think of nothing that would have a more disastrous effect than the resurrection of opposition in Quebec to acceptance of our Constitution. A Canada with a resentful Quebec refusing to cooperate under an imposed Constitution would be a crippled country." The Meech Lake Accord presented the only realistic chance of avoiding that situation.

The other major problem that had to be remedied was the imbalance in political power and influence that led Western Canada to feel that its interests were normally subordinated to those of the populous centre of Canada—Ontario and Quebec. Here the only thing that seemed likely to help was Senate reform. The reform would have to establish an elected Senate, of adequate power and authority, with substantially increased representation from the West. I said that "if it was important, as it was in 1968, to recognize that the federal arrangements and balance of 1867 were no longer acceptable to Quebec and French Canada, it is equally important now to recognize that the failure of the B.N.A. Act to give proper weight and representation to the West in our national Parliament is no longer acceptable to that region."

The essence of my argument was that, if Canada is to be able successfully to meet the complex challenges of the 21st century, it must first resolve some fundamental problems left over from the 19th. We have not done that. Our energies are constantly diverted from the problems ahead by conflict arising from institutions we have inherited from the past. Our unity of purpose and capacity for action dribble away because of unresolved issues at the very core of our national structure.

PREFACE

When I spoke on September 1, 1988, it looked as though the first of the two basic problems was on the way to resolution. Starting with the legislature of Quebec in June, 1987, and continuing to the second ratification by the House of Commons over objections by the Senate in June, 1988, the Meech Lake Accord had received the approval of nine of the 11 elected legislative assemblies of Canada whose approval was necessary. It now looks anything but sure that the Accord will receive the two remaining approvals in New Brunswick and Manitoba unless something new is added. Indeed one approval, that of Newfoundland, may be withdrawn again unless there is something new. The argument in this short volume is that the "something" cannot be re-opening the Constitutional Accord, 1987, as now approved in nine of the 11 legislatures. It should be parallel action on the other major problem—Senate reform. That would do something for the Western sense of grievance. It could also be attractive to New Brunswick and Newfoundland. Altogether, it might alter the psychological climate sufficiently to make agreement on the Accord possible.

Some attention to Senate reform, if it is to be serious and to carry conviction, cannot be provided in a few weeks or months, even if it were to be agreed upon as a necessary course of action at the Conference of First Ministers now scheduled for November, 1989. This raises the question whether there is, in fact, a time limit on approval of the Meech Lake Accord.

Official statements thus far have been that there is a time limit and that, if the Accord does not receive the approval of the legislatures of New Brunswick and Manitoba by June 23, 1990, three years from the first approval by the legislature of Quebec, it will die. I am convinced, as I said in my address of September 1, 1988, and in an earlier commentary at the meeting of the Council of Trustees of the IRPP in June, 1988, that there is no such time limit. Meech Lake will not die in June, 1990.

The argument as to why there is no time limit is tedious and legalistic. I have tried to state it as briefly and in as non-technical language as I could in Chapter 3. While I am a lawyer by training, I did not want to present an analysis so completely contrary to official statement and to accepted wisdom without the comfort of authority much greater than my own. I therefore put the argument before the Honourable Ronald Martland, who was a justice of the Supreme Court of Canada from 1958 until his retirement in 1982. Mr. Justice Martland has authorized me to say that he is in agreement with the opinion that the ratification of the Meech Lake Accord is not subject to any time limit.

To be certain of the situation, it would seem desirable for the Government of Canada to refer the matter to the Supreme Court. It is a simple, straight-forward question involving four sections of the Constitution Act, 1982: Sections 38, 39, 41 and 42. It should not be impossible to have the Court's opinion well before June, 1990. If the argument in Chapter 3 is found to be correct, there would then be ample time to see if a solution cannot be found to the problems now besetting the Meech Lake Accord—and also to the deeply felt dissatisfaction of the West, and of some of the Atlantic provinces, with our lack of a properly constituted second chamber in our national Parliament.

I have not, in this book, gone into the provisions of the Constitutional Accord, 1987, itself. These have been the subject of detailed analysis, thorough discussion and wide differences of view in the media and before a variety of committees over the last two years. I set out my own views in support of the Accord before the Special Joint Committee of the Senate and the House of Commons on August 5, 1987, and before the Select Committee on Constitutional Reform of the Legislative Assembly of Ontario on March 23, 1988. In essence, I told the Joint Committee that, in my judgement, the primary objective of policy with respect to the Constitution now is to achieve an arrangement under which Quebec can become a willing participant in the Canadian Confederation. The Accord, I said, would be undesirable, even if it could achieve that purpose, if its provisions would "involve consequences that are seriously adverse to Canada", and stated my opinion that they would not. The final question was "whether there is a reasonable prospect of getting better arrangements than those incorporated in the Constitutional Accord, 1987". Here one has to accept that any arrangement must be a compromise which will not totally meet the wishes or objectives of any government or legislature but which must, at the same time, be acceptable to all. I expressed the view that the 1987 arrangement "is probably as good as can be achieved" and that we are "most unlikely to get anything better". I remain of those views.

PREFACE

On Senate reform, I have gone into more detail because it has not been as widely discussed as the Constitutional Accord. As the structure for organizing my comments, I have used the three "E's" so generally supported in the West as the desirable characteristics of a new Senate: elected, equal (in provincial representation) and effective. Each of the three adjectives has to be examined in the light of the history and the nature of Canada, as well as the constraints imposed by our parliamentary system of government. I would not insist with confidence on any view advanced in the chapters on the Senate except that Senate reform is not worth the effort if it does not terminate appointment and substitute election as the basis of membership.

The final revisions of this book have been influenced by two visits to Quebec City in June and August, 1989, for meetings at which well-informed people from all provinces were present. Each meeting was focused on the outlook for Canada. It is apparent from the discussions and from the views expressed, that our difficulties as a country are much more profound than action on the Meech Lake Accord or on Senate reform as such. They involve growing feelings in Quebec, in the West and in the Atlantic region that other Canadians, elsewhere in Canada, do not understand their worries and their discontents and—what is more dangerous—do not want to try to understand. Words or arguments will not dissipate those impressions. What is needed is action. It is my hope that some of the proposals here may help to bring that about.

In the presentation of the arguments and proposals in this manuscript I have been helped by wise comments and criticism from friends and former colleagues. Hon. J.W. Pickersgill, Robert Bryce, Guy Roberge and Peter Dobell have all given me the benefit of their experience in parliamentary affairs and government. I am most grateful to them. They have no responsibility for any errors of fact or judgement in the final text.

I am also grateful to my wife for her criticism of form and expression in a legalistic document she must have found tedious beyond measure.

Gordon Robertson
Fellow-in-Residence
Institute for Research on Public Policy, Ottawa   September 1989

Préface

Au début de 1988, j'ai été invité à participer au congrès annuel de l'Institut d'administration publique du Canada, qui devait se tenir en septembre de la même année. Le thème devait porter sur les défis qui attendaient le Canada dans l'avenir, relativement aux problèmes qu'allaient poser "les impératifs de la concurrence mondiale". On me demandait de faire une présentation sur la manière dont notre système de gouvernement fédéral pourrait être adapté afin de faire face à ces défis. Après des réflexions préliminaires quant à la nécessité du fédéralisme pour un pays comme le Canada, régionalisé et divisé, j'ai fait remarquer que si on avait la possibilité de choisir un système de gouvernement doté d'un minimum d'efficacité pour répondre aux défis de la concurrence extérieure, ou même aux défis internes de gouvernement, à coup sûr on ne choisirait pas un système fédéral. Pourtant, le Canada ne peut pas exister sans un tel système. Les différences régionales et culturelles sont trop nombreuses pour que les Canadiens puissent faire totalement confiance à un gouvernement central unique. La question était donc de savoir que faire ou ne pas faire pour assurer notre survie et, si possible, notre prospérité, dans un monde de plus en plus concurrentiel, face à des problèmes sans cesse plus complexes, au pays comme à l'étranger.

J'ai suggéré qu'une première chose essentielle à faire était, au minimum, de mettre de l'ordre dans notre structure fédérale et ensuite de nous libérer de ces querelles constitutionnelles qui, au cours des vingt dernières années, ont tant accaparé l'attention, l'énergie et le temps de nos gouvernements, de nos dirigeants et de nos concitoyens.

J'ai dit qu'à mon avis notre système fédéral comportait deux faiblesses majeures auxquelles il fallait remédier, faute de quoi il n'y aurait pas moyen d'obtenir le consensus nécessaire pour que le pays puisse fonctionner sans s'exposer aux conflits qui trop souvent le détournent des véritables décisions politiques et tendent à nous faire oublier l'objectif national. J'ai dit que l'un de nos problèmes pricipaux venait du fait que la constitution avait été révisée en 1982 sans l'assentiment du Québec et que cette situation était inacceptable pour cette province. J'ai dit que "si nous avions l'intention d'éviter les différends susceptibles de diminuer l'efficacité du Canada dans les efforts entrepris pour faire face à la concurrence internationale, je ne pouvais imaginer rien de plus désastreux que la résurgence d'une opposition du Québec à l'égard de la constitution. Un Canada au sein duquel un Québec plein de ressentiment refuserait de coopérer dans le cadre d'une constitution qui lui aurait été imposée serait un pays diminué." J'ai ajouté que l'Accord du lac Meech présentait la seule possibilité réaliste d'éviter une telle situation.

L'autre problème à résoudre était celui du déséquilibre qui existe au sein du pouvoir et des influences politiques, situation qui a amené l'Ouest du Canada à avoir l'impression que ses intérêts étaient habituellement subordonnés à ceux des provinces plus peuplées du centre du Canada: l'Ontario et le Québec. Le seul remède possible à cette situation serait une réforme du sénat. Cette réforme devrait prévoir un sénat élu, doté des pouvoirs et de l'autorité nécessaires, où les représentants des provinces de l'Ouest seraient en plus grand nombre. J'ai dit que "s'il était important, comme c'était le cas en 1968, de reconnaître que l'organisation fédérale et le mécanisme d'équilibre de 1867 n'étaient plus acceptables pour le Québec et le Canada français, il devenait également important de reconnaître, aujourd'hui, que l'Acte de l'Amérique du Nord britannique, dans son impuissance à donner au Canada de l'Ouest l'influence et la représentation nécessaires au sein de notre parlement national, n'était plus acceptable pour cette région."

PRÉFACE

L'essentiel de mon argumentation était que, pour affronter avec succès les défis complexes du 21ème siècle, le Canada devait d'abord résoudre certains problèmes fondamentaux hérités du 19ème siècle. Cela reste encore à faire. Nos énergies sont sans cesse diverties des tâches nécessaires pour la préparation de l'avenir du fait des conflits engendrés par les institutions dont le passé nous a gratifiés. Nos efforts vers un but commun et notre capacité d'agir se trouvent paralysés du fait des questions restées sans solution au coeur même de notre structure nationale.

Lorsque j'ai pris la parole, le 1er septembre 1988, le premier de ces problèmes semblait sur le point d'être résolu. Après l'approbation de l'assemblée législative du Québec, en juin 1987, et la seconde ratification par la chambre des communes faisant suite aux objections du sénat, en juin 1988, l'Accord du lac Meech avait reçu l'approbation de neuf assemblées législatives élues sur les onze dont la ratification était nécessaire. Il semble maintenant peu probable que les deux provinces restantes, le Nouveau-Brunswick et le Manitoba, approuvent l'Accord, à moins qu'on y apporte certaines modifications. En fait, une autre ratification, celle de Terre-Neuve, risque également d'être remise en question, à moins de nouveaux développements. Ce que j'essaie de démontrer dans ce court volume, c'est que les "modifications" demandées ne peuvent pas être la remise en question de l'Accord constitutionnel de 1987 approuvé par neuf assemblées législatives sur onze. Ce devrait être plutôt une action concertée en vue de résoudre l'autre problème majeur, à savoir: la réforme du sénat. Cela permettrait d'alléger le ressentiment de l'Ouest à l'égard du Canada central. Cela pourrait également s'avérer intéressant pour le Nouveau-Brunswick et Terre-Neuve. À proprement parler, cela pourrait transformer le climat psychologique au point de rendre possible un consensus sur l'Accord du lac Meech.

Une réforme du sénat, si l'on veut qu'elle soit sérieuse et entraîne l'adhésion, ne peut se faire sans une attention suffisante. Quelques semaines ou même quelques mois ne suffiront pas, même si cette marche à suivre était décidée à la réunion des premiers ministres prévue pour novembre 1989. Reste donc à savoir si, oui ou non, l'approbation de l'Accord du lac Meech doit se faire avant une certaine date limite.

Jusqu'ici, les déclarations officielles font mention d'une date limite et précisent même que si l'Accord ne reçoit pas l'approbation des assemblées législatives du Nouveau-Brunswick et du Manitoba avant le 23 juin 1990, soit trois ans après la première approbation par l'assemblée du Québec, cet Accord deviendra caduc. Pour ma part, je suis convaincu, comme je l'ai indiqué dans ma déclaration du 1er septembre 1988 et dans un commentaire antérieur fait à la réunion de la Commission de direction de l'IRP en juin 1988, que cette date limite n'a pas lieu d'exister. L'Accord du lac Meech ne deviendra pas caduc en juin 1990.

Les raisons qui permettent de conclure à l'inexistence de cette date limite sont fastidieuses et relèvent de l'argumentation juridique. J'ai essayé d'en rendre compte aussi brièvement et aussi simplement que possible dans le chapitre 3. Bien que je sois juriste de formation, je n'ai pas voulu présenter une analyse si contraire aux déclarations officielles et à l'opinion commune sans avoir l'appui d'une autorité beaucoup plus importante que la mienne. J'ai donc soulevé cette question devant l'honorable Ronald Martland, ancien juge à la cour suprême du Canada, de 1958 à sa retraite en 1982. Monsieur le juge Martland m'a autorisé à dire qu'il était d'accord avec l'opinion que la ratification de l'Accord du lac Meech n'était pas assujettie à une date limite.

Pour en être tout à fait sûr, il serait bon que le gouvernement du Canada soumette la question à la Cour suprême. La question est relativement simple; elle ne met en cause que quatre articles de l'Acte constitutionnel de 1982, à savoir: les articles 38, 39, 41 et 42. L'opinion de la Cour devrait pouvoir être obtenue bien avant juin 1990. Si l'argumentation contenue dans le chapitre 3 du présent volume se révélait correcte, il y aurait alors amplement le temps d'examiner les moyens d'arriver à une solution des problèmes qui empêchent la réalisation de l'Accord du lac Meech, et aussi de trouver une formule susceptible d'apaiser le profond mécontentement de l'Ouest et de certaines provinces de l'Atlantique, dû au fait d'un sénat mal conçu.

Je n'ai pas, dans ce livre, abordé les clauses de l'Accord constitutionnel de 1987 lui-même. Au cours des deux dernières années, celles-ci ont fait l'objet d'analyses détaillées, de discussions approfondies et de considérables échanges de points de vue dans les médias et devant divers comités. J'ai commencé à présenter mes

PRÉFACE

propres arguments en faveur de l'Accord devant le comité spécial mixte du sénat et de la chambre des communes, le 5 août 1987, et devant le comité d'enquête sur la réforme constitutionnelle de l'assemblée législative de l'Ontario, le 23 mars 1988. En bref, j'ai déclaré au comité mixte que, selon mon opinion, l'objectif principal, en ce qui concerne la constitution, devait être de parvenir à un accord qui permettrait au Québec de devenir un participant de son plein gré au sein de la confédération canadienne. Toutefois, ai-je dit, même s'il atteignait cet objectif, l'Accord resterait indésirable si les clauses du document "avaient pour conséquence d'aller sérieusement à l'encontre des intérêts du Canada", et j'ai ajouté que je ne pensais pas que ce soit le cas. La dernière question était de savoir "s'il existait quelque chance de pouvoir parvenir à s'entendre sur des mesures meilleures que celles qui figurent dans l'Accord constitutionnel de 1987." À ce stade, il faut admettre le principe que toute mesure doit être le résultat d'un compromis qui, par définition, ne pourra être exactement conforme aux souhaits et objectifs de tous les gouvernements ou de toutes les assemblées législatives, mais qui pourra malgré tout être acceptable pour tous. J'ai exprimé l'opinion que l'accord de 1987 "était probablement aussi satisfaisant que possible" et que nous ne pourrions "vraisemblablement pas espérer quoi que ce soit de meilleur." Je persiste dans cette opinion.

En ce qui concerne la réforme du sénat, je suis entré plus avant dans les détails du fait que celle-ci n'a pas fait l'objet de débats approfondis comme c'est le cas de l'Accord constitutionnel. Quant à la présentation de mes commentaires, j'ai suivi les trois revendications généralement soutenues par l'Ouest pour justifier la nécessité de réformer le sénat, à savoir: un sénat élu, l'égalité de représentation des provinces et une efficacité réelle de cette institution. Chacun de ces objectifs doit être examiné en fonction de l'histoire et de la nature du Canada, compte tenu des contraintes auxquelles notre système de gouvernement parlementaire est soumis. Avant d'insister avec assurance sur l'un quelconque des arguments avancés dans les chapitres sur le sénat, je tiens à préciser qu'une réforme du sénat ne vaut pas la peine d'être entreprise si elle ne met pas fin au système de nomination et ne lui substitue pas le principe de l'élection pour le recrutement de ses membres.

A HOUSE DIVIDED

La mise au point définitive de ce livre a été influencée par deux visites que j'ai faites à Québec en juin et en août 1989, pour participer à des rencontres qui rassemblaient des gens bien informés de toutes les provinces. Chacune de ces réunions avait pour objet l'avenir du Canada. Des discussions et des points de vue exprimés, il ressort que nos différends sont profonds et dépassent largement telle ou telle action que nous pourrions prendre à l'égard de l'Accord du lac Meech ou d'une réforme du sénat. Au Québec, dans l'Ouest et dans la région de l'Atlantique, on a de plus en plus le sentiment que les autres Canadiens ne comprennent pas les préoccupations et le mécontentement de ces régions et, qui plus est, et ceci est beaucoup plus dangereux, qu'ils ne font aucun effort pour les comprendre. Ce ne sont ni les mots ni les raisonnements qui parviendront à dissiper ces impressions. Ce qui importe, c'est d'agir. J'ai espoir que certaines des propositions présentées ici pourront aider à sortir de cette impasse.

Lors de l'élaboration des arguments et des propositions que je présente dans ce manuscrit, j'ai été aidé par les sages conseils et les critiques éclairées d'un certain nombre d'amis et d'anciens collègues. L'honorable J.W. Pickersgill, Robert Bryce, Guy Roberge et Peter Dobell m'ont tous fait profiter de leur expérience en matière d'affaires parlementaires et gouvernementales. Je leur en suis profondément reconnaissant. Ils ne sont nullement responsables des erreurs de fait ou de jugement du texte définitif.

Je suis également reconnaissant à ma femme pour ses critiques sur la forme et l'expression d'un document qui relève de l'argumentation juridique et qui a dû lui sembler ennuyant au possible.

Gordon Robertson
Chercheur émérite
Institut de recherches politiques, Ottawa   Septembre 1989

The Author

Gordon Robertson has had as long a connection with federal-provincial and constitutional questions as anyone in Canada. Under Prime Minister St. Laurent, he organized the two Constitutional Conferences in 1950 that tried to devise a procedure for amending the Constitution of Canada. He was principal adviser to Prime Minister Pearson for the conference in 1964 and for the one in February 1968, that launched the discussions that lasted, with many vicissitudes through the Trudeau regime to the "patriation" of the Constitution in April, 1982. For ten years, until his retirement from the federal public service in 1979, Mr. Robertson was Chairman of the Continuing Committee of federal and provincial officials on the Constitution.

Mr. Robertson is a lawyer by training, with a law degree from Oxford University. After entering the Public Service of Canada in the Department of External Affairs, he served in the Office of the Prime Minister (1945-48) and the Privy Council Office (1949-53) before being appointed Deputy Minister of Northern Affairs and National Resources in 1953. He held that position, as well as being Commissioner of the Northwest Territories, until 1963, in which year he was appointed Clerk of the Privy Council and Secretary to the Cabinet. In 1975, in response to increasing constitutional and federal-provincial problems, he was named to a new position, that of Secretary to the

Cabinet for Federal-Provincial Relations, to devote full time to those issues.

Mr. Robertson retired from the Public Service in 1979 and became President of the Institute for Research on Public Policy in the following year. Since his retirement from that position in 1984, he has been a fellow-in-residence of the Institute. In 1982 he was made a member of the Queen's Privy Council for Canada. He is a Companion of the Order of Canada and Chancellor of Carleton University.

Mr. Robertson has spoken and written widely on questions relating to public policy, including language problems, federal-provincial relations, and the Constitution.

Chapter 1

The West and the Senate Problem

Agreement on the Senate was the key to Confederation in 1867: agreement on its reform could be the key to the impasse that today threatens the renewal of our federalism for the future.

It is in the West that the need for senate change is most strongly held. It has, however, become of increasing interest in the Atlantic provinces. There is no cause for surprise that there should be little awareness of the issue in Ontario and Quebec. Those provinces, when their interests coincide, hold the preponderance of power in Confederation by reason of their dominance of population. The 1981 census puts the population of central Canada at just over 15 million out of a total population of 24.3 million: nearly 62 per cent. The system of distribution of seats in the House of Commons modifies the strict application of population arithmetic in that chamber. At present Ontario and Quebec have 174 seats out of 295: a shade less then 59 per cent. The four Western provinces together have 86 seats: 29 per cent. Ontario is at ease with our federal structure. While Quebec is not, none of its discomforts can be removed by Senate reform. The centre of Canada is in the "comfortable pew" so far as our Parliament is concerned.

A HOUSE DIVIDED

There is nothing unusual in an imbalance of population among regions of a federation. Indeed, the reason a federation exists at all is because different parts of a country, especially a sprawling one like Canada, have major differences, of which population size is often one. Those differences are the basis of the two essential characteristics of a federal system: the establishment of two orders of government, one central and the others regional, and the structuring of the central government to provide protection within it for the smaller, the less numerous or the linguistically or ethnically "different" regions of the country.

It was the United States, in the constitution worked out among the representatives meeting at Philadelphia in 1787, that found the second chamber in the legislature to be the place to achieve a balance, in the new national government they hoped to establish, between the large, populous states on the one hand and the smaller, less populous ones on the other. After months of difference and near collapse of the discussions, the "great compromise" on the two houses of Congress made agreement possible. In the House of Representatives there would be representation of the states according to their population. In the Senate, to protect the smaller ones, states would have equal representation: two from each, regardless of population. Without that compromise, a constitution and the union of the states would almost certainly not have emerged.

The Fathers of Confederation, in their meetings at Charlottetown and Quebec in 1864, were well aware of the basic problem and of the American solution. As R.A. Mackay says in his classic work, *The Unreformed Senate of Canada,* "The importance of this question in the minds of the statesmen at Quebec may be gleaned from the fact that practically the whole of six days out of a total of fourteen spent in discussing the details of the scheme were given over to the problem of constituting the second chamber". The three colonies in the Maritimes wanted protection against too great dominance of the new federal Parliament by Ontario and Quebec: the "Canada" of that day. Quebec, with its special cultural and linguistic situation, had an equal but different interest: protection against the greater English-speaking population of all the other parts of the prospective union. In spite of the American precedent, only Prince Edward Island pressed for provincial equality in the second chamber. It was agreed that there

2

should, instead, be regional equality among "Three Divisions" of Canada: 24 senators for each of the regions coming into Confederation—Upper Canada (Ontario), Lower Canada (Quebec) and the Maritime colonies (initially Nova Scotia and New Brunswick, with Prince Edward Island added in 1872).

There were no western provinces to argue for any western protection in 1867. Manitoba became a tiny province with two senators in 1870. British Columbia was brought in by Imperial Order in Council in 1871. Alberta and Saskatchewan were carved out of the Northwest Territories in 1905. All had small populations at the beginning. It was not until 1915 that a full "western region" was established with 24 senators, six from each western province. The Three Divisions of 1867 constitutionally became four at that time. The basic regional equality established in 1867 and completed in 1915, was, in a typically Canadian way, ignored without being formally modified when Newfoundland became a province in 1949. It was given six senators, producing an "Atlantic region" of 30. However, the constitutional provision that the "four Divisions shall—be equally represented in the Senate" was left unchanged.

Over the years, dissatisfaction of the West with the arithmetic of Senate representation increased. Westerners saw, year after year and regardless of the government in power, a House of Commons dominated by the representation of "central Canada". However, far from having a second chamber that could qualify this imbalance, westerners saw a Senate in which the "central region" of Ontario and Quebec had 48 seats while the West had only 24. In western eyes there was and is neither provincial nor genuine regional equality to offset the preponderance of population in the industrialized and prosperous centre of Canada.

It is not, however, primarily the numerical balance that has undermined the Senate in its essential federal purpose of providing special representation for our less populous regions in the structure of central government in Canada. It is the fact that, from the beginning in 1867, the method of selecting senators has meant that they have no genuine authority to represent or to speak for the provinces or the regions from which they come. As R.A. Mackay put it in 1926, speaking of the weakness of the Senate in the Canadian political structure:

3

The cause (i.e. of the Senate's weakness) is undoubtedly that it has no political foundation. As Mill pointed out over a century ago, "An Assembly which does not rest on the basis of some great power in the country is ineffectual against one which does." The House of Commons rests upon the electorate, the Prime Minister and his Cabinet rest upon the majority in the House of Commons, the Senate rests upon nothing but itself and the Prime Minister or party leader who has appointed its members. Intended to represent the interests of the various sections and provinces, it was deprived of any real representative character by reason of the fact that the sections and provinces were given no hand in the appointment of its members. (p. 159)

Mackay's conclusion of 1926 is as valid in 1988: "the Canadian Senate as a House of Parliament represents nothing." Representing nothing, it is not surprising that it has failed to establish itself as the effective voice of regional interests that the Fathers of Confederation talked about and that the underlying conditions of federalism require.

The near equality of the Senate's legal powers to those of the House of Commons was nullified in practice by its realization at an early date that it could, only at the risk of its own destruction, pretend to rival the elected House. It has rarely taken the chance of flexing the muscles that the Constitution formally gave it. The limited respect our Senate originally enjoyed has steadily diminished as public tolerance for patronage appointments in general has decreased. Patronage is no longer acceptable in Canada as the basis for a legislative chamber any more than is the property qualification that was also, in 1867, made a requirement for senatorial appointment. That qualification still exists—a relic of another age. The defects in the original design, and the lessened respect for a body based on patronage alone, has meant that the Canadian federation has lacked one of the two essential features of federalism. We are alone among democratic federations in that respect and our lack explains many of the problems that have plagued our federal system increasingly in recent years.

There are only two ways in which the members of a second chamber can be chosen today if they are to be able to speak with recognized authority for the regions they are supposed to represent. One method is by election: the other is by appointment by the government or the legislature of the region or state from which they come. The Constitution of the United States in 1787 provided that two senators should be chosen by the legislature of each state. In 1913 the Seventeenth Amendment changed the system to direct election. In Switzerland and Australia the choice is also by popular vote. The Federal Republic of Germany has the other method: designation by the state governments. In their case, the representatives in the second chamber are ministers of the state government itself.

Only Prince Edward Island pressed for election of the members of the senate at the Quebec Conference of 1864. The Province of Canada had an elected Legislative Council from 1856. It had not been a great success and the delegates from Canada did not advocate the electoral basis for the second chamber in the new federation. With regard to direct election, Mackay says:

> The chief objections to it were that it tended to create two houses of exactly the same character which were both likely to consider themselves the interpreters of the popular will, and that such a condition would inevitably lead to conflicts between the houses. In addition, it was un-British. (p. 42)

The preamble to the British North America Act, 1867, which established the new federation, said that the three "provinces" had "expressed their desire to be federally united under the Crown of the United Kingdom of Great Britain and Ireland, with a Constitution similar in principle to that of the United Kingdom." It is possible that more attention was focused on the British constitution and ensuring the "similarity of principle" than on the implications of being "federally united". The British Parliament had two chambers, the "second" being made up of hereditary peers and bishops of the established Church of England. The source of their status, either immediately or historically, was the Crown. The closest approach in the circumstances of Canada was appointment by an Order in Council approved by the representative of the Crown in Canada, the Governor General. That type of appointment had been normal for the pre-Confederation colonial legislative councils, except for the brief experiment with election after 1856 in Canada. The fact that the appointed Councils had notoriously been creatures of the governor or of the government that appointed them, and that such an appointment,

5

essentially by the Prime Minister of the federal government, would create a Senate of a character inconsistent with the implications of being "federally united", does not appear to have got much consideration.

It was not long after the West began to be settled that the sense developed that western interests were different from those of "the East". St-James Street and later Toronto were the demons: the financial interests that influenced governments, set interest rates and took extortion from the returns to western agriculture in transportation charges and in the prices of farm implements. Under Sir John Macdonald's National Policy, with its protective tariffs to shelter "eastern" industry, the western farmer paid the protected prices that made Massey-Harris plants profitable in Ontario. With no protection whatever, the farmer received the world price for his grain, whatever it might be. It made for a precarious life on the prairies and the difference from eastern protection and comfort was resented.

The sense of grievance and of impotence in the West has been one of the constants of Canadian history. It reached its apogee with the National Energy Policy of the Trudeau government in the 1980s. Having suffered under low world prices for wheat and high domestic prices for manufactures for all their history, western provinces were now told that the rules had changed. They were *not* to get high world prices for their oil and gas because that would injure householders and industries in "the East". The divergence of regional interest within the federation was as stark as was the incapacity of the West to have its voice effectively heard in parliament or by government in Canada.

The frustration of Western Canada at what it perceives as its lack of hearing in the Parliament of Canada and its inadequate influence on national policies is embittered by the sense that the region, as a whole, has been for most of the period since the Second World War a net contributor to the financing of Confederation. This has not always been so. During the pre-war years of depression and drought the Prairie provinces had to receive special assistance from Canada as a whole. They could not finance in the poverty of the time and the Canadian federal system had no established basis for assisting poor regions to provide even minimal services to their citizens in times of extreme depression. From that experience of acute distress in some provinces came the decision to appoint the Royal Commission on

Dominion-Provincial Relations. In 1940 it recommended a system of national adjustment grants "designed to make it possible for every province to provide, for its people, services of average Canadian standards." Special arrangements covered the war and the immediate post-war period, but in 1957 an arrangement similar in principle to the Royal Commission's recommendation was instituted as "equalization". That program has come to be what some have referred to as the "glue" that holds Canada together. In 1982 it was incorporated into the Constitution.

While the prairies were the area of greatest need before the war, it is the eastern part of Canada that is the region that has consistently received equalization payments since they were established in 1957. The balance varies year by year as economic conditions change but the Atlantic provinces are invariable receivers of the largest equalization payments per capita. Quebec has also been a normal receiver of equalization, although at a lower rate in relation to population than the Atlantic region. British Columbia and later Alberta have consistently had revenues from their own taxes that have been above the national average so they normally receive no equalization payments, nor does Ontario, the other net provider of funds in the national balance of tax payments. The situation of Manitoba and Saskatchewan has varied, depending mainly on crop conditions and world agricultural prices. While it may, as the Bible says, be more blessed to give than to receive, the West is more aware of having given, year in year out, than of any form of blessing or even of recognition for that contributor's role within the federation. It would be wrong to say the West begrudges equalization. It needed it acutely 50 years ago when equalization did not exist. Some parts of the West still need it from time to time. But it is galling to have been for so long the net giver financially and at the same time to have had so little recognition of Western grievances and so little influence on the policies of the state.

The establishment of the Reform Party of Canada in 1987 was, its constitution states, "born out of the discontents and frustrated aspirations of Western Canadians." A year later, in the election of 1988, the party took 15 per cent of the vote in Alberta and finished second in nine of the province's 26 ridings. Across the West it won about 9 per cent of the vote. In 1989 it elected its first Member of Parliament in a by-election in Alberta.

It is too soon to know what lasting success the Reform Party may have. In 1920 the National Progressive Party was founded, also based on western grievances as felt at that time. Its immediate success was much greater: a total of 65 seats in the election of 1921. In the three Prairie provinces it won 38 seats out of 42, leaving the Liberals with two and the Conservatives with none. The leadership of the Progressive Party was no match for the political astuteness of Mackenzie King and its success was ephemeral. Its program, many of its members and most of its supporters were gradually absorbed into the Liberal party. In the elections of 1930 it won only two seats in the West against 20 for the Liberals, out of a total of 48 western seats. Western grievances continued for a time to be voiced by the United Farmers of Alberta, who won ten seats in 1930, and later, by the Social Credit Movement. These too have disappeared as national parties, although some would argue that a vestige lives on in British Columbia.

It would be rash and unwise to assume that western political protest will again, as in the 1920s and 1930s, dwindle and disappear if little or nothing is done to meet western dissatisfaction. Indeed, the two subjects with which this study deals—Senate reform and Meech Lake—were the first two planks in the "election platform" of the Reform Party in November, 1988: for the Senate, a "Triple E Senate"; for the Meech Lake Accord, its rejection.

While the West could and did punish the Liberal Party from 1974 onward for ignoring western interests, and while the Mulroney government after 1984 was more sensitive to western views, the awarding by it of the CF-18 contract to a Montreal company, for a more expensive and technically inferior bid than the one submitted by a Winnipeg company, convinced many westerners that no adequate protection for the West would be available until something new was added to the federal balance. It is too easy for federal governments, even friendly ones, to prefer "the East" with 174 House of Commons seats over the West with 86. The main focus of western interest in constitutional change has become a senate with a new regional balance—a "triple E Senate": elected, effective and equal in representation from every province.

Chapter 2

The Morass of Meech Lake

Canada's most acute preoccupation and problem in the last 20 years has not been that of western frustration. It has been to find a solution to the crisis that was identified by the Royal Commission on Bilingualism and Biculturalism in its Preliminary Report of February 1, 1965. The Commission had held hearings throughout Canada in the 18 months following its appointment in July, 1963. The meetings with Canadians in all their variety in all parts of the country had come as a shock to the commissioners, who had thought they were probing questions simply of language and of relations between linguistic groups. They said:

> The Commissioners, like all Canadians who read news-papers, fully expected to find themselves confronted by tensions and conflicts. They knew that there have been strains throughout the history of Confederation; and that difficulties can be expected in a country where cultures exist side by side. What the Commissioners have discovered little by little, however, is very different: they have been driven to the conclusion that Canada, without being fully conscious of the fact, is passing through the greatest crisis in its history.

The Commission found that "the source of the crisis lies in the Province of Quebec" where ". . . the state of affairs established in 1867, and never since seriously challenged, is now for the first time being rejected by the French Canadians of Quebec". It was only three years later that the warning took on a new urgency with the establishment of the Parti Québécois dedicated to the separation of Quebec from Canada.

The constitutional discussions, launched by Prime Minister Pearson in February, 1968, were intended to address the "deficiencies" that had been revealed in the arrangements embodied in the British North America Act in 1867 as they had been "translated into action and practice" over the years. "The one that has assumed the greatest dimension is the dissatisfaction of the people of Canada of the French language and culture", according to Mr. Pearson in the official statement of his government's position: "Federation for the Future". The statement went on:

> It is the intention of the Government of Canada, with which it hopes the governments of the provinces will concur, that this Conference of February 1968 should mark the beginning of a process of constitutional review that will be both broad and deep. If we are to be sure that we have the best arrangements we can devise to order and to govern the relationships between Canadians in the Canada of the future we must be willing and concerned to examine all of the facets of our legal framework. The Government of Canada is ready to undertake such a total review. (p.4)

The provinces did concur in "a process of constitutional review . . . to examine all the facets of our legal framework". Meetings were held among First Ministers, Ministers responsible for various aspects of constitution and policy, and officials who handled preparatory work and tackled points of detail. All governments had an awareness that there was a genuine urgency in finding some means to modify the framework of the federation and the operations under it that had produced such serious tensions.

The difficulties and frustrations of the process from 1968 to the failure of the Victoria Conference in 1971, and in further efforts from 1973 to 1975, appeared to vindicate the claim of the Parti Québécois that Confederation could not be reformed: only separation would make possible the "flowering" of Quebec as a modern French-speaking society, secure in its culture and language for the future. Its argument proved convincing. The P.Q. was elected to office in Quebec in November, 1976, with separation as its objective: the crisis was clear.

Still further efforts to achieve agreement on constitutional change in 1977 and 1978 failed. The failures prepared the way for the Quebec referendum in May, 1980. The question in the referendum was whether a mandate should be given to the government of Quebec to negotiate "sovereignty-association" with Canada—political sovereignty combined with economic association. What it contemplated, and what it really asked the people of Quebec to authorize, was the establishment of a separate state of Quebec.

It is hard to know to what extent the "no" vote in Quebec, which in the end won the referendum, was influenced by the promise that a "no" vote would *not* be a vote for the *status quo*. The *status quo* had no support in French-speaking Quebec, even among federalists there. The promise on the federalist side from Canadian leaders from other provinces than Quebec, as well as from Ottawa, was that there would be a "renewed federalism". Prime Minister Trudeau affirmed in a major address that he and his government would "change the Constitution" if Quebecers rejected the sovereignty option.

What did "change" and "renewed federalism" mean? Mr. Trudeau argues that he, as prime minister, had always defined change as "patriation" of the Constitution and a Charter of Rights—exactly what he delivered at the Constitutional Conference of November 1981, and in the Constitution Act, 1982. There can be no question about Mr. Trudeau's own position: he had consistently resisted changes that he thought would weaken a strong central government for Canada. There is equally little doubt, however, but that the political parties of Quebec at the provincial level, and probably many voters in Quebec, did not understand the promise that way in the context of the referendum campaign of 1980. They clearly expected some adjustment in some directions that Quebec governments had sought during the previous decade. Mr. Lévesque, as premier, walked out of the 1981 constitutional conference when the final agreement was one among the federal government and the other nine provinces: the government of Quebec was not a party to its conclusions. All parties in the legislature of Quebec later voted to condemn the "agreement without

Quebec". The position that Quebec would not consent to the Constitution was made clear, despite its legally binding character for the province. In April, 1982, Canada had a changed Constitution: but not one that French-speaking Quebec saw as the "renewal" they thought they had been promised. The Constitution was changed in a way rejected by all Quebec provincial parties. Their resentment at the imposition of the Constitution was clearly shared by most of the French-speaking people of the province.

The election of Mr. Mulroney's government in September, 1984, and of Mr. Bourassa's Liberal government in Quebec in December 1985, provided the chance to see if some way could not be found by which Quebec could, as Mr. Mulroney put it, accept the Constitution "with honour". The government of Quebec, in May, 1986, produced five points that constituted the things it thought essential for constitutional reform. The five were a program of change much more modest than had been advanced by any government of Quebec in the long and depressing history of constitutional discussion from 1968 to 1981. The Quebec proposals became the basis of the Meech Lake Accord of April 30, 1987. In the legal form of the "Constitutional Accord" of June 3, 1987, the agreement was approved by the legislature of Quebec three weeks later. The Parliament of Canada and the legislatures of seven other provinces followed in succeeding months up to July, 1988.

As this is written in September, 1989, it is by no means clear that the Meech Lake Accord will become law. Unanimous consent of the provincial legislatures is required as the Accord includes two changes that are among the items listed in Section 41 of the Constitution Act, 1982, as requiring unanimity. New Brunswick and Manitoba, with governments elected to office after the Meech Lake Accord was agreed to in 1987, have not yet given their approval. The new government of Newfoundland threatens to withdraw the approval given by the pre-election legislature.

So far as Western hopes for Senate reform are concerned, Meech Lake has become a morass—whether it is approved or not.

Senate reform was no part of Quebec's "five points" of May, 1986. That province, like Ontario, has never evinced much interest in the question. It was Premier Getty of Alberta who most of all wanted assurance that, once the problem of Quebec's "exclusion" from the Constitution had been remedied,—which all provincial premiers had agreed in August, 1986, had to be the priority issue—Senate reform would be addressed. Unfortunately, the provisions Mr. Getty agreed to in the Accord make the achievement of his objective more difficult if Meech Lake is, in the end, approved by New Brunswick and Manitoba and comes into effect.

Mr. Getty's first mistake was in accepting any element of Senate reform whatever as a part of Meech Lake. Resting as it has done since 1867 on unadulterated prime ministerial patronage, the present Senate is indefensible as an institution of federalism. No rational argument can be made that it can, as it stands, discharge the essential role of a second chamber in a federation. The Senate will achieve a faint tincture of legitimacy as a voice of regional interests if that federal patronage is diluted by recommendation from a province for a nomination to fill a Senate vacancy. That is the "temporary" reform Mr. Getty agreed to "until an amendment to the Constitution of Canada is made in relation to the Senate".

Mr. Getty's second mistake was in allowing Senate reform to be included among the items added to the list of things that require unanimous consent for constitutional change. That is done in the proposed new Section 41(b) and (c). At present the powers of the Senate, the method of selecting senators and the "number of members by which a province is entitled to be represented in the Senate" can be changed with the agreement of two-thirds of the provinces with "at least fifty per cent of the population of all the provinces". (Section 38 of the Constitution Act, 1982). Once Meech Lake is approved, the consent of all will be required. Any province will be able to prevent senate reform if it is unhappy about any part of it.

In short, Meech Lake, if passed in order to solve one of our federal problems—the fact that Quebec will not consent to our Constitution as it stands—will make the solution of our other federal problem—the lack of a satisfactory second chamber—extremely difficult. The only thing worse for solution of that second problem is if Meech Lake does not pass at all.

If Meech Lake is not approved, Mr. Bourassa's government will almost certainly not agree to change the Accord to meet the criticisms that have been levelled against it. It represents that government's minimum position, and the government has been much attacked in Quebec for setting the minimum too low. It would be politically fatal to touch the "distinct society clause" or to try to trim any of the five points of 1986. The only alternative government of Quebec in the foreseeable future would be one formed by the Parti Québécois. Its minimum for any agreement would probably be some form of separation from Canada. And with no agreement, no government of Quebec would participate in any way in any constitutional change. Senate reform would become impossible. However difficult Senate reform may become with Meech Lake in effect, there is at least the possibility of change. Without it, it is doubtful if the possibility exists at all for many years to come.

Chapter 3

The Myth of the Time Limit

Spokesmen for the Government of Canada and for some of the provinces have frequently stated that the Meech Lake Accord will die unless it receives the unanimous consent of the provinces by June, 1990. The media have slavishly repeated that solemn sentence of death like a mantra. It is almost certainly wrong.

The assertion that there is a three year time limit for Meech Lake rests on Section 39(2) of the Constitution Act, 1982.[1] The general amending provision for our Constitution is Section 38. It sets forth the consent requirements that must be met before an amendment under it "may be made by proclamation by the Governor General issued under the Great seal of Canada". Section 39(2) then provides:

> A proclamation shall not be issued under Section 38(1) after the expiration of three years from the adoption of the resolution initiating the amendment procedure thereunder.

---

1. The text of Part V of the Constitution Act, 1982, which sets forth the procedures to be used in amending the Constitution of Canada, is in Appendix A. All the Sections referred to in this chapter are contained in Part V.

The amendment procedure is initiated by the first formal resolution approved by either the Parliament of Canada or the legislature of a province. The first resolution in the case of the Constitution Amendment, 1987, was passed by the legislature of Quebec on June 23, 1987. Three years from that date, June 23, 1990, has thus been asserted to be the day that Meech Lake dies if unanimous consent of the provinces has not been secured in order to permit a proclamation to be issued by that time.

The only problem is that the time limit in Section 39(2) refers specifically to Section 38. The amending procedure for the Meech Lake Accord has not been taken under Section 38 and could not be. The "motion for a resolution to authorize an amendment to the Constitution of Canada" that is the instrument for the formal approvals by Parliament and by the legislatures is specific in two paragraphs of its recital about the need to act under Section 41. The reason is simple: two parts of the amendments included in the Meech Lake Accord deal with matters that can be amended only with the unanimous consent of all provincial legislatures. These relate to the composition of the Supreme Court and a change in the amending procedure. It is Section 41, not Section 38, that deals with amendments requiring unanimous consent. There is no time limit for an amendment made under Section 41.

It is not too hard to discern what may have been the reason in 1982 for making a difference in this respect between Section 38 and Section 41. Section 38 makes provision for amendments to the Constitution without the unanimous agreement of all the provinces. Such amendments can be effected if they receive the assent of Parliament and of at least two-thirds of the provinces that have, in the aggregate, at least 50 per cent of the population of all the provinces. It was apparently felt to be reasonable that amendments that could be made without the unanimous consent of all the provinces should be effected within a specific period of time after the inception of the amendment procedure. There is, however, no logical reason why an amendment to the Constitution which has the unanimous assent of all the provinces, and therefore on which there is no differing view among the governments and legislatures, should be subject to any such restriction.

THE MYTH OF THE TIME LIMIT

The only argument that can be made against application of these clear provisions of the Constitution, and of the logic that explains the limitation of the time restriction to Section 38 alone, relates to Section 42.

Section 42(1) of the Constitution Act, 1982, provides that amendments relating to certain matters "may be made *only* in accordance with subsection 38(1)". Among the matters listed in Section 42 are two that may be considered to be affected by the Meech Lake Accord: the method of selecting senators (for the temporary nominating arrangement) and the Supreme Court of Canada—although the latter is doubtful, since the "composition of the Supreme Court" comes, as indicated above, specifically under Section 41 and is excepted from Section 42. The question is, however, whether Section 42(1) means what it says. Can the matters it lists be amended only under Section 38(1) and *not* under Section 41?

It seems clear that Section 42(1) cannot mean what it appears to say. The consequence of interpreting it literally would be nonsense. In effect it would amount to the proposition that changes that can be made under Section 38, with the agreement of 2/3 of the provinces having 50 per cent of the population, cannot be made under Section 41, with the agreement of all the provinces with 100 per cent of the population. That ludicrous result could not have been intended. Section 41 requires everything that Section 38 does in the way of consent and approval and a good deal more. To prefer Section 38, and to exclude Section 41, would be absurd. What, then, could Section 42(1) mean?

The purpose of Section 42(1) may be related to two other parts of the total amending procedure that is set out in the Constitution Act, 1982: Sections 43 and 44. Its intent could be to ensure that those sections could not be used to circumvent the requirements for approval that are established in Section 38. There would be reason and purpose for such a provision.

Section 43 permits an amendment "that applies to one or more, but not all, provinces" to be made with the authorization of Parliament and "the legislative assembly of each province to which the amendment applies". Section 43 specifically permits an "alteration to boundaries between provinces" with the approval of Parliament and the legislatures of those provinces only. Conceivably another province might feel concerned about such a change even if the amendment did not apply to it and thus did not involve its approval. Section 42 has a provision that relates to provincial boundaries. It says that only Section 38 can be used with respect to "the extension of existing provinces into the territories". Without Section 42 the fear might be that the boundaries of one or of two provinces might be changed to add parts of the present territories to it or to them without the agreement of other provinces. This was in fact done for Ontario, Quebec and Manitoba in 1912. Very large parts of the Northwest Territories of that day were added to those provinces to the annoyance of the Maritime provinces, which were not consulted. The fear could be that Section 43 might be used, if Section 42 were not there, to evade the general consent requirements of Section 38 for such territorial extensions of some present provinces without all provinces being involved. This is not an improbable concern in the light of what happened in 1912.

Section 44 deals with another category of constitutional change. It permits amendment of the Constitution of Canada "in relation to the executive government of Canada or the Senate and House of Commons" by the Parliament of Canada alone. However, that power is made specifically subject to Section 42. By reason of its being so subject, three matters relating to the Senate and House of Commons cannot be amended by Parliament alone under Section 44 but "only" under Section 38 with the approval of 2/3 of the provinces.

In brief, there may have been a purpose in Section 42, but the purpose cannot have been to exclude the use of Section 41 from amendment of the matters it says "may be made only in accordance with Subsection 38(1)". The irrationality of interpreting Section 42 to exclude Section 41 is made the clearer when it is realized that the entire change made by Meech Lake to the amending procedure is to put *all* the items thus far listed in Section 42 as being amendable "only in accordance with Section 38(1)" into Section 41. In the Constitution of Canada as revised by the Meech Lake Accord, Section 42 will no longer exist. It is apparent that whatever purpose it was meant to have in 1982 was marginal and unimportant. Certainly it was not intended to exclude amendments by unanimous consent under Section 41 or, through Section 39(2), to put a time limit on them.

THE MYTH OF THE TIME LIMIT

That the three-year time limit in Section 39 does not apply to the Meech Lake Accord seems beyond reasonable doubt. However, for any who may have trouble with the precise wording of Section 42 and the literal reading of "only", it is worth pointing out that the requirements of Section 38, to which Section 39 applies, were met many months ago.

Section 38 requires the approval of Parliament and of 2/3 (i.e., seven) of the legislatures in provinces that contain 50 per cent of the population of all the provinces. Instead of the minimum of seven provincial legislatures, Meech Lake has received the approval of eight. The eight provinces involved contain 92.8 per cent of the population of all the provinces according to the 1981 census. Any conceivable argument about a need to comply with Section 38 has already been met, well within the three years Section 39 prescribes.

This is not to suggest that the relevant parts of the Accord should now be proclaimed. Meech Lake is an indivisible whole: a total package, of which one or two parts cannot be divided off for separate action. But this fact brings us back to the original point. Since the Accord is a package, it must be approved by the procedure necessary for whatever part or parts of the package require the highest level of approval. That "highest level" is unanimity of the legislatures of all the provinces. Constitutional changes that require unanimity must be made pursuant to Section 41 and this is what is being done.

Stating the argument in summary form, the time limit imposed by Section 39 applies to amendments made pursuant to Section 38 and to those only. The amendment for the Meech Lake Accord is not being made under Section 38 and it could not be. It is being made pursuant to Section 41. There is no time limit on action under that section. Any amendment to the Constitution under Section 41 may be effected without any limit of time provided the unanimous consent of all the provinces is obtained.

The consequence of there being no time limit may be of great importance if the governments of Manitoba and New Brunswick judge that they are not in position to recommend to their legislatures approval of the Meech Lake Accord, as it stands or alone, by June of 1990.

The process in which Canada is involved, of trying to achieve the renewal of federalism that will meet the "rejection" by French Canada of the present arrangements of which the Royal Commission on

Bilingualism and Biculturalism spoke in its report of 1965, has been under way since February, 1968—for more than 20 years. The apparent commitment of Canada to such renewal to meet Quebec's problems was undoubtedly a factor in the victory of the federalist forces in Quebec in the referendum on separation in 1980. That success avoided the possible tragedy of a fracture of our Canadian union. The Constitution Act, 1982, with the Canadian Charter of Rights, was a great accomplishment—but Quebec was left outside. It was not a "renewal" that carried conviction there.

The proposals of the Bourassa government four years later, in May, 1986, constituted more modest changes than had been proposed by any previous government of the province—Liberal, Union Nationale or Parti Québécois. Agreement by the First Ministers at Meech Lake on the principles that became the Constitutional Accord, 1987, was another major accomplishment. It has received the approval of nine of the 11 elected assemblies of the people of Canada whose approval is constitutionally necessary. Twenty years and more of effort should not be lost or prejudiced by ill-timed or unwise efforts to meet a constitutional clock unless it is certain that the clock is really ticking in this further stage of constitutional reform. Meech Lake is not the first change designed to adjust a 120 year old Constitution to new facts and new forces, and it will not be the last, unless what has been done and gained so far is thrown away by unnecessary haste. It is a matter of acute importance whether the alleged constitutional demise is fact or fiction. The consequence of death by the clock in June, 1990, would almost certainly be an impasse that would make impossible any constitutional reform or any constitutional cooperation for many years to come.

Since so much has been said about a time limit for Meech Lake and since it is so crucial, the wise course would appear to be for the Government of Canada to refer the question to the Supreme Court. Only the opinion of the Court can remove the doubt. If the argument here is correct, an opinion that there is not a time limit, and that the Meech Lake Accord will not die in June, 1990, will provide the time that may be needed to permit the careful consideration by our government leaders and by the people of Canada of the best means finally to achieve the renewal of our federalism that has eluded us for so long.

Chapter 4

The Common Interest of the West and Quebec

The prospects for approval of the Meech Lake Accord by the legislative assembly of Manitoba are bleak.

The loss of power by the New Democratic Party government of Mr. Howard Pawley in the election of April, 1988, and its replacement by a Progressive Conservative government under Mr. Gary Filmon, did not necessarily imperil the Accord. The Federal Conservative Party, led by Mr. Mulroney, had made the achievement of an agreement with Quebec a central theme in the campaign leading to its victory in the election of 1984. Mr. Filmon and his provincial party appeared, after assuming office in 1988, simply to be waiting for a favourable moment to secure approval of the Accord by the legislature. That approval was initially considered likely to be forthcoming even though the government was in a minority. The NDP had formed the previous government which had signed the Meech Lake Accord for Manitoba. With their support, Mr. Filmon's government could out-vote the Liberals, led by Mrs. Carstairs, who were strongly opposed to the Accord. Several things changed the picture in the late months of 1988.

Manitoba, since its establishment as a province in 1870, has had a troubled history of relations between the two language groups and in the handling of language issues. Mr. Pawley was undoubtedly straining the limits of good will among his English-speaking electors when he committed his government, in 1987, to an agreement that recognized Quebec as a "distinct society". It was not too improbable to link the NDP loss of public support and of power in the election just a year later to popular disapproval of some parts of the Accord. Mr. Pawley's successor as NDP leader, Mr. Gary Doer, had not been directly involved in the Meech Lake agreement and had no personal commitment to it. The re-election of Mr. Mulroney's government on November 20, 1988, which meant that the Free Trade Agreement with the United States would go into effect, and its approval in December by Parliament, gave Mr. Doer a basis for withdrawing the support of the NDP for the Accord.

The Meech Lake Accord had been attacked, especially in the West, for the provision that will permit a provincial government, under certain conditions, to opt out of future national shared-cost programs in areas of exclusive provincial jurisdiction and to receive "reasonable compensation" in doing so. The provision was seen as undermining the federal government's capacity to mount nation-wide programs, especially for social security, with common benefits and standards across the country. A similar concern was felt about the Free Trade Agreement. It was charged that it would endanger the "Canadian way" in health, welfare and social security: such programs would be imperiled as Canada was drawn closer to the market-dominated philosophy of the United States and as competition became sharper with free trade. A week after the federal election, Mr. Doer linked the two risks to national social programs: together they were too great a threat to the policies the New Democratic Party espoused. His party, he announced, had changed its position on the Meech Lake Accord. Unless the Accord was amended, the NDP would oppose its approval by the legislature of Manitoba.

With the government in a minority in the legislature, the loss of NDP support was fatal. However, during December, 1988, the noisy dispute in Quebec over the use of the English language on signs brought another problem. It re-awakened the Manitoba sensitivity over anything relating to language and culture. The outrage at Premier Bourassa's use of the "notwithstanding clause" in Section 33 of the Charter of Rights to ensure the constitutionality of Bill 178, with its exclusion of the use of the English language on outside signs in Quebec, made any attempt to approve the Meech Lake Accord in Manitoba even more hazardous politically. The year ended with the announcement by Premier Filmon that his government would not proceed with the resolution of approval in the legislature. It was clearly a decision of political realism. There is no prospect of approval with the government in its present minority position: the arithmetic in the legislature cannot be disputed.

It seems unlikely that the problem can be resolved by a provincial election at any early date. There is little comprehension in Manitoba, or in the West generally, of the concern in Quebec for the future of the French language and culture in that province. Nor is there any understanding of the symbolism that is involved, especially in Montreal, in outside signs as a part of the visible "face of Quebec" to proclaim to all that Quebec and Montreal are, indeed, French—as French as other provinces and cities in Canada are English. Having that face French is felt to be psychologically important in the effort to resist the steady encroachment of the English-speaking sea of over 200 million that surrounds Quebec in North America. Without that understanding, the "language of signs" policy appears petty and vengeful: the method of imposing it, a confession of violation of individual human rights. The concept, so important in Quebec, of collective rights for a linguistic minority that does not have the protections that a separate country could provide, is also neither understood nor accepted. As a result, the implications of the recognition of Quebec as a "distinct society", and of the requirement to interpret the Constitution in future "in a manner consistent with" that recognition, both of which are a part of Meech Lake, have taken on a baleful cast in Manitoba eyes. Almost certainly any election there in the near future would find the Accord a controversial issue. That clause, as well as other provisions in the Meech Lake Accord, have been strongly attacked in hearings by the committee of the legislature on the Accord. Unless something new is added that can change the climate in the province, it is difficult to see any party gaining a majority in Manitoba with a program that includes approval of Meech Lake.

One thing that might improve the prospects for the Meech Lake Accord in the West generally, and in Manitoba where the immediate problem is, would be if the government—and the people—of Quebec recognizes that the West too is dissatisfied with the way Confederation and our Constitution have worked thus far.

It is understandable that Quebec should be very conscious of its own problems within the Canadian union. It was legitimate to insist, as Premier Bourassa did, that first priority should be given to modifying the Constitution of Canada as it stands after the Constitution Act, 1982, to remedy the most important deficiencies left by the exclusion of Quebec from the 1981 agreement. Prime Minister Mulroney accepted that priority in 1984 and his government has adhered to it since. The governments of all the provinces also subscribed to the priority at the Interprovincial Conference in the summer of 1986. The priority was the basis for the urgent attention that was given by the governments to Quebec's "five points" in the fall and winter of 1986-87. It was honoured, to the point of physical exhaustion, in the meetings of First Ministers at Meech Lake in April and in Ottawa in June of 1987. The priority of the Quebec problem was also preserved in action by every government that had been involved in the Accord itself. The only governments that have not yet proceeded with approval by their legislatures are the two that were not in office in 1987 and did not participate in the agreement. What is needed now is for the government of Quebec to show greater understanding of political realities in those provinces and of the existence of problems in the rest of Canada, and in the West especially.

It would be both an overstatement and an understatement to suggest that the assessment of the Royal Commission on Bilingualism and Biculturalism in 1965 with regard to "the French Canadians of Quebec" can be applied to the West—that the "state of affairs established in 1867, and never seriously challenged, is now for the first time being rejected". The "state of affairs" in the West was established progressively from 1870 to the amendment to the British North America Act in 1915 in which the West became a fourth region for Senate membership. The constitutional and political situation as perceived by the West has been increasingly challenged for many years, to the point where it is not an exaggeration to say that it is now "rejected" by many of its people and leaders. This is as little understood in Quebec as the threat to the future of the French language and culture in Quebec is understood in the West.

THE COMMON INTEREST OF THE WEST AND QUEBEC

The basic complaint of the West is that the essential facts of Canadian population and economic strength, which put the greatest power in the central provinces of Ontario and Quebec, are not offset by the political structure of Confederation as is normal in federations, but rather are augmented by that structure. The parliamentary system, which requires that the government have the confidence of the House of Commons and be subject to daily challenge in it, requires collective responsibility for all policy by the Cabinet and strict party discipline in the House. The result is that western interests and views, constantly in a minority in both Cabinet and Commons, receive little reflection in policy and no significant expression in the elected chamber of Parliament. The role of the House of Commons is not to be a forum for regional views but rather to support the government or, in the case of the opposition, to attack its policies and actions. There is little room for discussion that does not stick to the party line. The Senate, as it has been since Confederation, operates to worsen the situation. The distribution of seats gives the centre of Canada twice as many seats as the West. The lack of any representative basis for senators means that those who come from the West cannot be an authoritative voice for western interests.

The proof of the western grievance about the lack of western influence is demonstrated in the fact that its constitutional problem has received so little attention over so many years. It has tended to be dismissed as a rustic eccentricity: something of no consequence and deserving of no serious attention. Quebec's legitimate grievance of 1982 received prompt and energetic attention. The contrast has not been unobserved in the West. It adds to the frustration and irritation.

An interesting question is why the West, with a total population of 7.2 million in the census of 1981 and 86 seats in the House of Commons in 1988, has not been able to get attention for its constitutional problem while Quebec, with a smaller French-speaking population of 5.3 million and only 75 seats in the House of Commons, has been able to do so. The difference between the emotional intensity of the sense of injustice to Quebec's French language and culture, on the one hand, and the more diffuse anger over western political subordination, on the other, is undoubtedly a factor. There is greater unanimity and stronger feeling in Quebec on its cultural issue than there is in the West about its frustration. Moreover, Quebec has a single, strong government to give voice to its concerns. In the West, four governments with differing priorities and views and differing electoral timetables make a clear focus of pressure impossible. At the level of national politics, French-speaking Quebec presents a greater homogeneity and a greater sense of shared concern over readily definable interests than the West does. As a result, it is both easier and also more important for national political parties to shape their programs in a way that will respond to Quebec's concerns. There are undoubtedly other factors but, whatever the reasons, the results are clear. Quebec has secured national attention for its constitutional problem: the West has not.

Thus far there has been no indication by the political leaders of Quebec of any awareness of legitimate constitutional problems anywhere else in Canada. Some words, and especially some actions, to convey that recognition could be important in creating the conditions in which the Meech Lake Accord could receive the provincial approvals it now lacks. If it is accepted that there is no time limit on approval of the Accord, a year or two spent on a problem of priority to the West, and of importance for the Atlantic provinces as well, might involve no real loss of time as, without such attention, there is little prospect of approval, especially in Manitoba, at any early date. A concession by Quebec in that respect could be what is needed to unblock the present stalemate that, if not resolved, may endanger the prospects for achieving its priority: the removal of the unacceptable humiliation of being legally bound by constitutional changes imposed on Quebec in 1982 without its consent.

Concealed by the mutual frustrations and irritations of Quebec and the West is a common interest. Each wants the Constitution of Canada modified in ways it thinks important to create a regime that will be more just and equitable for the future. Neither can achieve its objective without cooperation from the other.

Polls taken in Quebec consistently show that a majority want Quebec to remain a part of Canada. An Angus Reid poll taken in January, 1989, found 63 per cent of francophones in Quebec opposed to independence. With equal consistency polls show English-speaking Canada even more opposed to the idea of Quebec leaving Confederation. In the same poll only 28 per cent favoured that possibility in the Prairie provinces where acceptance of Quebec's possible departure is strongest. Two thirds of Canadians supported the proposition that "Canada is a bilingual country with both English and French as official languages". We are not faced by a condition in which the majority of Canadians in the West want to see a continued dissatisfaction of Quebec with the Constitution. What they want is some equal attention to their own dissatisfaction.

A sense that Quebec has sympathy with the frustrations and problems of the West could lead to more understanding of and sympathy for the concerns of Quebec. A convincing start on the process of Senate reform might alter the climate that now prevents a government or legislature in Manitoba from approving the Meech Lake Accord. It could also make a significant difference in the other two points of danger—New Brunswick and Newfoundland.

Chapter 5

The First "E": An Elected Senate

The three most comprehensive studies in recent years of the problem of Senate reform as the means of achieving effective regional representation in the Parliament of Canada have agreed that the Senate should be elected.

The first report, *Regional Representation: the Canadian Partnership*, was sponsored by the Canada West Foundation and appeared in 1981. It exhaustively examined alternative models in the federations and the various proposals that had been made in Canada for Senate reform, especially during the 20 years preceding. The essential recommendation of the report was that "The resolution of the problem of effective regional representation in Canada be sought by establishing an elected Senate" and that "members of the Senate of Canada should be directly elected for limited terms." In support of its recommendation the study said:

> The reasons for considering direct election flow, not from any alleged tidal wave of democratization to which we must automatically yield, but from the practical and immediate implications of election. An individual who holds his position because he has been elected to that position has a clear and unambiguous mandate to represent those people

who elected him in matters directly pertaining to the issues and concerns that emerged as significant during that election. Election for a limited term implies a clear and direct accountability to those voters at the end of that term. The result of the combination of these two factors is legitimacy. (p. 108)

A Special Joint Committee on Senate Reform was established by the House of Commons and the Senate and held hearings from May to October, 1983. It reported in January, 1984. Its central conclusion was essentially the same as that of the Canada West report:

We have concluded that the Canadian Senate should be elected directly by the people of Canada.

An appointed Senate no longer meets the needs of the Canadian federation. An elected Senate is the only kind of Senate that can adequately fill what we think should be its principal role—the role of regional representation. We propose a Senate different in composition and function from the House of Commons and from the present Senate. The second chamber we recommend is designed specifically—by its distribution of seats, by the way it is elected, and by the powers it exercises—to represent the sometimes diverse interests of the people of Canada's provinces and territories in federal legislation and federal policies.

In fulfilling that role, an elected Senate would strengthen the authority of Parliament to speak and act on behalf of Canadians in all parts of the country. (p. 1)

The Special Joint Committee's report differed from the Canada West study in the manner of election, the term of office of senators and the distribution of Senate seats among the provinces, but on the fact that direct election was the only satisfactory basis for the Senate it was in agreement. So was the third major study: that of the Legislature of Alberta. It established a Select Special Committee on Senate Reform in November, 1983, which reported in March, 1985. The Committee recommended that "The Senate of Canada should maintain as its primary purpose the objective established by the Fathers of Confederation, namely to represent the regions in the federal decision-making process". The problem, it said, was that "the Upper House does not have the faith of the Canadian public" primarily "because of the method of appointment". The Committee had found in its hearings that "Canadians want a system in which they have a direct relationship with their Senator". The report went on to say:

> The Committee came to the unanimous conclusion that an elected Senate for Canada is essential for a necessary balance in the system of government. The need for an effective provincial voice in the federal legislative process is long overdue. If steps are not taken to satisfy this void in the process of government, there may be serious repercussions. The only possible conclusion was to recommend a directly-elected Senate. (p.24)

The Royal Commission on the Economic Union and Development Prospects for Canada (the Macdonald Commission), appointed in November, 1982, focused primarily on "the appropriate national goals and policies for economic development" but it was also directed to examine and report on "the appropriate institutional and constitutional arrangements to promote the liberty and well-being of Canadians". It was to "take account of, and respect, the spirit of the Constitution of Canada and assume a continuing Canadian federal structure not significantly different from its present form". In Volume Three of its report in 1985 the Commission addressed "three basic and closely related objectives" to strengthen "the capacity of Canada's institutional arrangements to accommodate the internal social, economic and political diversity found within Canadian society". The Commission commented that Canadians think of representation in our political institutions in regional or provincial terms and that, as a consequence, "representation in national institutions must be thought of not only as the representation of individuals, but also as the representation of regional or provincial interests". There was a "tension" between the concept of equal representation of individuals and representation of the provinces with smaller populations. The Commission continued:

> The questions raised by these issues are complex and difficult. The fact remains, however, that in recent years, by any measure of regional representation, our national institutions have been seriously flawed. It is not an

exaggeration to speak of an institutional failure which has had profound consequences for the governance of Canada.

What are the dimensions of this failure? Despite the importance of regional differences in Canada, the present design of our national institutions gives remarkably little attention to regional interests. Federal systems around the world typically represent regional interests, not only through the division of powers between central and state or provincial governments, but also through the representation of provinces or states within the national government. In the original U.S. constitution, for example, states had equal representation in the Senate, and Senators were named by state legislatures. In West Germany, the second Chamber, the Bundesrat, is made up of ministers of state governments.

In Canada, where we draw on the British tradition of parliamentary government, we have built our federalism primarily on the division of powers. Our nation is, perhaps, unique among federal systems in our relative exclusion of the representation of regional interests from the centre. (Vol. 3, p.72)

The Commission concluded that it was not desirable "to modify the basic principle of representation by population, on which the House of Commons is properly constituted," but it was desirable "to make the parliamentary caucus of our parties more representative of Canada's regions". The report went on:

Our proposed solution attempts to meet both these concerns by moving to an elected Senate where membership is weighted towards the smaller provinces, and where election is based on proportional representation. This change will simultaneously strengthen the position of the less populous provinces in the joint Senate-House of Commons caucus of the parties, and also contribute, through proportional representation, to a distribution of those caucus members in each party which is closer than the present arrangement to their actual electoral support in the regions.

These modifications must be made in ways consistent with the tenets of responsible government. (Vol. 3, p. 82)

THE FIRST "E": AN ELECTED SENATE

The essential points of these four reports, all of which agree on the importance of an elected senate as a means of solving problems in the Canadian federal structure, are set out in tabular form in Appendix B. They differ on the method of election recommended. The two reports by members of our legislative bodies are reluctant to depart from our traditional system: the "first-past-the-post" plan. The other two reports advocate a more innovative reform based on proportional representation.

The Commonwealth of Australia, a federation that resembles Canada in having a parliamentary system of government, started with a "first-past-the-post" system of election for their Senate and, after 18 years, changed to proportional representation. Their experience with an elected senate over more than 80 years is instructive as to things to emulate and also things to avoid. The best study of it from a Canadian perspective was made by Professor Donald Smiley of York University for the Institute of Intergovernmental Relations at Queen's University and published in 1985: *An Elected Senate for Canada? Clues From the Australian Experience.*

With 12 senators from each state, half the senators are elected every three years, which is the Australian term for their House of Representatives. For the senatorial election under the Single Transferable Vote system, each state is a single constituency. So far as the voter is concerned, the process is simply that of indicating by numbers his or her preferences among the candidates: not much more complex than marking our "X". It is the counting of the ballots that is complicated, but this problem is for the election officials.

The essentials of the system, once the ballots have been cast, start with a count, in each state, of the total number of first choices. That total is then divided by one more than the total number of candidates to be elected (six plus one, in the Australian case). The resulting number, plus one, becomes the "quota" for election.

Any candidate who receives a total of first preferences equal to or greater than the quota is elected. Any surplus votes the candidate received are then "transferred" to other candidates in proportion to the second preferences on all the ballots that gave first preference to the successful candidate. If no candidate gets a quota of first preference votes, or if none has a quota after the transfer of second choices, the candidate with the fewest votes is dropped. His or her second choices are then distributed to the remaining candidates. By this process of distributing next preferences from candidates who reach the quota and from those with the fewest votes, stage by stage, quotas are gradually achieved on the basis of the preferences the voters have declared. When five candidates have achieved quotas, the candidate among those remaining who receives a majority of the votes is declared elected, notwithstanding that number of votes he or she has received is not equal to the quota. The slate of six elected senators is thus complete. The process ensures that the six are those who have received the highest level of preference among all the voters of the state.

In explaining its preference for this system for Canada, the report of the Canada West Foundation said:

> The principal advantage of the system is that it allows the voter to fine-tune his own electoral choice. He can decide for himself whether he wants his support to go to a particular party, or only to a specific individual regardless of party affiliation. Even when he decides to support a particular political party, he can choose which candidate of that party he prefers. This flexibility on the part of the voter encourages a similar flexibility on the part of the candidate, who must now make clear to the voters what he stands for. The Transferable Vote allows the voter to choose, not just one party over another, but one individual over another. (p. 117)

As Professor Smiley says, "The aim of all P.R. systems is to facilitate the choosing of an assembly which mirrors electoral opinion more exactly than do the results of the first-past-the-post procedure". The Macdonald Commission analyzed the results of the 1984 federal election to compare the percentage of the vote received by each party by province and the number of seats in the House of Commons each one secured. It then did a projected distribution of seats in an elected Senate with proportional representation. The two tables are set out in Appendix C. The differences in the total number of seats for the three parties are dramatic. In the House of Commons, with the first-past-the-post system, the Progressive Conservative Party received one of the largest majorities in Canadian history: 211 seats out of 282. In a Senate elected by P.R. it would have received a bare majority. The Liberal Party and the New Democratic Party would each have had some representation in the elected Senate from every province, except Prince Edward Island in the case of the N.D.P. In brief, the projected results for 1984 demonstrate the difference that can be made by a system of proportional representation in "mirroring electoral opinion more exactly" than our traditional system of voting does.

The Canada West report analyzed what would have been the composition of an elected Senate over the past two decades using the distribution of seats in the present Senate, with elections at the same time as federal general elections and assuming that people voted for candidates of the same party for both Commons and Senate. The results in all cases were very different from the returns to the House of Commons. Although the government would almost always have had the largest group in such an elected Senate, it would never have had an absolute majority in any election in that period. The result in 1984, after the Canada West study, was clearly exceptional. This normal minority situation for a Senate elected by P.R. has major implications for the powers to be given to such a Senate if governmental instability is to be avoided and if the principle of responsibility to the House of Commons alone is to be preserved. This is discussed further in Chapter 7.

A related and complex question is the way in which the structure of the Single Transferable Vote system should be designed to have participation by the political parties, which is essential for effective elections, without putting so much power in the hands of the parties that their influence will curb the active expression of independent regional views. Smiley comments that, in Australia, "Despite the apparent anti-party bias of the PR-STV system, the Australian parties have gone a very long distance in establishing party dominance over the process by which members of the Senate are chosen". The Australian experience suggests both things to do and things to avoid in trying to get party involvement without party domination.

Based on his study of the Australian system, Professor Smiley concludes:

> So far as the system for electing Senators is concerned, there is little to be said for a first-past-the-post system for electing members of a new Canadian Senate. According to this procedure voters would put crosses beside the names of Senators to be elected in each province up to the number of

such persons to be chosen. Particularly if Senate elections coincided with those for members of the House of Commons this would almost inevitably result in the same party balance in both chambers, as happened in the earlier period in Australia, and the Senate would be in large measure redundant. (p. 54)

Smiley ends with the further comment:

Current debate about a reformed Canadian Senate is preoccupied with provincial and regional representation. Yet apart from this, the adoption of any one of the variants of PR for choosing such a body might well have an effect on the enhanced representation of women, members of minority ethnic groups and so on as the parties worked to balance their respective tickets. (p. 55)

It is the argument of redundancy that is most conclusive against the "first-past-the-post" recommendation of the Joint Senate-House of Commons Committee and of the Alberta Committee. The argument of the former, that the Australian system would be "unfamiliar" to Canadian voters, is not persuasive. Its comment that "experience shows that election results are only marginally different from those under the present system" does not accord with the results in Australia or the hypothetical results in the Canada West study or in Appendix C.

"Unfamiliarity" is also the main burden of the argument of the Alberta Committee against proportional representation. The report comments that "The Canadian tradition of election practices leans toward the first-past-the-post system. ... the Committee strongly recommends major changes to Canada's federal system of government. Those changes are radical enough without injecting further change into the system at this time."

In the case of both committee reports it would appear that the comfort of the familiar system prevailed over the logic that flows from moving to an elected Senate at all. The Joint Senate-House of Commons Committee rightly says that the "principal role" for our second chamber is "to represent the sometimes diverse interests of the people of Canada's provinces". That role calls for a system that will indeed "represent", not for one that will inevitably distort as the first-past-the-post system does. Our traditional system of voting has a

compelling logic for the House of Commons. Proportional representation for election of Members of Parliament would make majorities in
that House virtually impossible. The result would be to make
government unstable and uncertain in a world where stability, within
a democratic system, is vitally important. There is no such argument
in favour of the first-past-the-post system, or against proportional
representation, for a Senate that is to represent views but specifically
is not to control the lives and fates of governments.

There could be an argument for having senators elected from
single member constituencies if the single transferable vote were used
for their election. This might provide a greater degree of proportionality than the present system but not as much or as certainly as
election with multiple member constituencies. On the other hand, it
would have the advantage of ensuring a measure of local identification
without which most senators might tend to come from the largest
population centres in each province. This matter is discussed further
in Chapter 8.

Chapter 6

The Limits to Equality

Western proposals for Senate reform have uniformly pressed for equal representation of all provinces. The report of the Canada West Foundation says:

> It is only in Canadian politics that the principle of equal representation for all provinces regardless of population is regarded as radical or unusual. Other federal systems (Australia, the United States, Switzerland) possess upper chambers whose members are drawn in equal numbers from each constituent unit, regardless of the differences in population. These systems accept as legitimate the dual nature of the representation that is required in a federal system: the representation of citizens in the national legislative process on the basis of both population and region. (p. 110)

To create a legislative chamber of "credible size" the report recommends that each province should have from six to 10 senators. The Alberta Select Special Committee was in agreement. It favoured six senators from each province and two from each Territory. The Special Joint Committee of the Senate and House of Commons heard a number of witnesses, especially in the West and in the Atlantic provinces, arguing for equality. In the end, however, the Committee recommended a different distribution.

After noting that there is equality for states and cantons, regardless of population, in the three federations referred to by the Canada West study, the report of the Committee continues:

> We note, however, that in none of these three federations is the imbalance between the constituent units as pronounced as it is in Canada. For example, Canada's largest province, Ontario, has about 36 per cent of the country's population; in the United States, the largest state has only about 10 per cent. In Canada, the application of the equality principle would enable the five least populous provinces—that is, those accounting for 13.4 per cent of the Canadian population—to have a majority in the Senate if they had the support of the territorial representatives, whatever their number. A resident of Prince Edward Island would have as much electoral clout as 70 Ontarians and 50 Quebecers. Such pronounced inequities could jeopardize the institution's credibility. Moreover, if this system were adopted, the only province with a francophone majority would see its relative weight in the Senate, which stood at 33 per cent of the seats in 1867 and today stands at 23 per cent, plummet to less than 10 per cent. (p. 28)

The Committee noted that in two other democratic federations, India and West Germany, "the equality principle has been weighted on the basis of the population of each state". It concluded that a distribution among the provinces on that basis would "reflect the Canadian reality more accurately than simple numerical equality can do". The report continues:

> For this reason, most members of the Committee favoured the following distribution: Ontario and Quebec would retain the same number of seats that they have now (24), and the other provinces would be given 12 seats each, with the exception of Prince Edward Island, which would be given 6. Yukon and the Northwest Territories would both have increased representation. This formula would produce a Senate with 144 members. The stronger role envisaged for the Senate both in regional representation and in committee work warrants a significant increase in the number of senators. (p. 29)

In effect, the Committee recommendation embodies the principle of equality for all provinces not at the extreme limits of population size: the largest two and the smallest one.

The Royal Commission on the Economic Union and Development Prospects for Canada, undoubtedly influenced to some degree by the Joint Committee report, arrived at the same conclusion about the distribution of Senate seats. After raising the question whether each province should have equal representation in the Senate, the report answers:

> We do not go so far: our objective is simply to establish a greater weight of influence for less populous regions relative to the more populous. In intergovernmental relations, provincial governments are, and should be, equal, a state which reflects their juridical equality and their responsibility for governing their respective provinces. Yet our institutional arrangements also recognize differences among the provinces to serve certain purposes. For some constitutional amendments, for example, size and number of provinces are combined to establish a voting formula. In our national government, where representation by region takes place within a single jurisdiction, a comparable adjustment is also appropriate. We wish to temper, not overrule, representation by population. (p. 88)

The reasoning and the conclusions of the Joint Committee and the Royal Commission are persuasive. An important part of the "Canadian reality", to which the Joint Committee refers, is that Canada recognizes two official languages and that, according to the 1981 census, nearly 85 per cent of the population of Canada whose mother tongue is French resides in one province: Quebec. A second chamber in a federation has, as its essential purpose, the adequate representation of the less numerous elements that make up the federation. This is done primarily on the basis of geography: by special representation in the second chamber for the regions or states. However, in a federation involving two major linguistic groups, adequate representation of the less numerous group is as important as the regional balance. It was a fundamental consideration in 1867 and the situation today, so far as the French-speaking population of

Quebec is concerned, places them even more in a minority in Canada that they were when Confederation was established.

In 1867, with the equality of three regions of that day, Quebec was given one-third of the Senate seats. At present is has 24 seats out of 104: 23 per cent. It would not be in accord with Canadian reality, Canadian history or the basic principles of federalism to expect that Quebec, with its enormous proportion of the French-speaking population of the country, could accept a reduction to 10 per cent of membership in the Senate. While there would undoubtedly be two or three French-speaking Senators from other provinces, the English-speaking element of the country would have close to 90 per cent of the seats. The linguistic balance would become far more disproportionate than the regional balance is today.

The distribution recommended by the Joint Committee and the Royal Commission would involve a major correction in the regional representation. The West, from having half the seats of the two central provinces together, would achieve equality with them: 48 from the West and 48 from the centre. The four Atlantic provinces would not quite achieve equality with Ontario and Quebec: 42 seats as compared with 48. However, there would be a substantial gain for the Atlantic region since it now has only 30 seats. Newfoundland, which has suffered the same inadequate representation as the Western provinces, would, like each of them, double its representation from six to 12.

Altogether, the distribution recommended by the Special Joint Committee in 1984 goes as far in the direction of equality as is consistent with the facts and the history of Canada. It would achieve the necessary correction in the regional balance of membership in the Senate without substantially upsetting the linguistic balance. Depending on what is done about the "Senate floor" for representation in the House of Commons (which is discussed in Chapter 8), it could further add to the representation in that chamber from the smallest and least prosperous of our provinces, the four in the Atlantic region. It is difficult to see any distribution more constructive, or more likely to appear reasonable to all provinces.

Chapter 7

Effectiveness within the Parliamentary System

The nature of our system of parliamentary government will shape the attributes necessary and possible to achieve effectiveness in an elected Senate for Canada.

Under our system, the government is responsible to the House of Commons. By constitutional convention, a prime minister must resign and his Cabinet leave office, or he must recommend a dissolution of Parliament and a new election, if he and his government lose the confidence of the House. It would not be possible, with an elected Senate, simply to leave the powers of our Senate as they now are: legally equal to the powers of the House of Commons except on appropriations of public money and the imposition of taxes or imposts. An elected Senate would and should use its powers to the full, however they may be defined. The situation in which our Senate has had powers that are virtually equal in law to the House has been workable only because senators have recognized that, in fact, whenever there is a contest of wills, the Senate must, in the end, yield to the elected House of Commons. There is no convention of government responsibility to the Senate: only to the House.

The study by the Canada West Foundation had no doubts that the parliamentary system is operable only if the government is, as now, responsible to one legislative body and not to two. The report said, in 1981:

> The existence of an elected Senate should not qualify in any way the principle or the operation of responsible government. The government of Canada should be responsible to the House of Commons, and should be required to retain the confidence of that body that duly represents the citizens of Canada on the basis of representation by population. The government of the day should not be responsible to both Houses in the sense of requiring the confidence of both to survive in office. The idea of "double responsibility" is not workable. Only in the House of Commons should a motion of non-confidence have any meaning; such a motion should have no place in the proceedings of an elected Senate.

> On similar logic, a money bill should be initiated only by a Minister of the Crown and only in the House of Commons. It is a fundamental principle of Anglo-American democracy (and not only of parliamentary systems, as the same rule applies to the American Congressional system) that money bills should be capable of being introduced only in the chamber that is based on representation by population. (p.117).

The Canada West report concluded that:

> With regard to both questions of confidence and money bills, the elected Senate of Canada should explicitly and by formal constitutional stipulation be subordinate to the House of Commons. (p. 118).

The Special Joint Committee of the Senate and the House of Commons was of the same view. The report of the Alberta Committee and that of the Macdonald Commission are not specific on the point of responsibility as such but their agreement with the other two reports is implied in what they recommend about Senate powers on money bills being limited so deadlock with the House of Commons cannot occur.

The special importance of money bills was made clear in Australia in 1975 when the refusal of its Senate to pass such a bill precipitated a constitutional crisis in which the government was brought down.

A Labour government, led by Prime Minister Whitlam, had been returned to office in an election in 1974. It had a majority in the House of Representatives, but not in the elected Senate. Professor Smiley sets out the essentials of the 1975 crisis:

> In September and October 1975 the Opposition forces decided to use their majority in the Senate to force the government to an early election and, when appropriation bills came before the Senate, that body declined to pass those bills unless the government agreed to such an election, a course of action that Prime Minister Whitlam and his party refused to take. On November 11 the Governor General dismissed the government and installed in its place a caretaker government under the former Opposition leader Malcolm Fraser under the condition that the new ministry would not introduce new legislative measures into Parliament prior to a general election. On the same day the Senate granted supply and Parliament was dissolved.... (p.14).

The consequence of the Australian Senate having a full veto power over money bills was the same in that crisis as if it had the power to withdraw confidence from the government and so directly affect its tenure of office.

In the light of the Australian experience, the Special Joint Committee of the Senate and the House of Commons recommended that the powers of an elected Senate in Canada should be defined with care so as to avoid the possibility of deadlock. In the Committee's view, this meant that the Senate should have only a suspensive veto in respect of general legislation, and no power even of delay in the case of money bills. The conclusion is of such importance that it is worth presenting at length:

> We therefore decided that it was wiser and more in keeping with the character of parliamentary government to give the Senate the power to delay but not altogether prevent the adoption of measures voted by the House of Commons. The Senate would therefore have a suspensive veto of a maximum of 120 sitting days, divided into two equal periods

of 60 days. Supply bills would not be subject to any delay. The mechanism we have in mind would work as follows:

(a)   Bills passed by the House of Commons would be transmitted without delay to the Senate.

(b)   Within the 60 sitting days following the transmission of a bill from the House, the Senate would make a final decision on it, either adopting it, rejecting it, or passing it with amendments. If the Senate had not made a final decision on a bill within the prescribed delay period, the bill could be presented direct to the Governor General for royal assent.

(c)   A bill adopted by the House of Commons and rejected by the Senate could not be presented to the Governor General for assent unless the House of Commons had adopted the bill a second time. That second adoption could not take place unless at least 60 sitting days had elapsed since the Senate rejected the bill.

(d)   If the Senate amended a bill passed by the House of Commons, the amendments would be transmitted to the Commons, which would have to accept or reject the amendments. If accepted, the bill could then be presented immediately to the Governor General for assent; if rejected, the bill could be presented to the Governor General for assent only after at least 60 sitting days had elapsed since transmission of the Senate amendments to the House. At the end of the 60-day period, the House would again vote on the amendments and on the bill. This rule would also apply to bills on which the House had rejected some Senate amendments while accepting others.

(e)   In computing the 60-day periods referred to above, only days when either House is sitting would be counted.

We decided to use sitting days rather than calendar days to avoid the distortions due to holidays and recesses. In practice, and depending on the time of the year, the maximum length of the delay would be between seven and nine months.

The business of supply has unique importance in our parliamentary tradition. A simple delay in voting the estimates can paralyse public administration for months. We regard this possibility as unacceptable. To give the Senate even a suspensive veto in such a vital area would amount to giving it a disguised power to overturn the government. We therefore propose that the Senate have no power over appropriation bills (including the main, interim and supplementary estimates). (p. 30).

The conclusions of the Macdonald Commission were substantially the same as those of the Special Joint Committee. The report reads:

An elected Senate which actually used the powers of the present Senate to initiate, veto and amend legislation could indeed complicate responsible government. Moreover, a government with a majority in the Commons might seldom have a Senate majority. Commissioners believe, accordingly, that with the exception noted below, the Senate should have a suspensive veto of six months on all ordinary legislation. This period should prove ample for it to consider fully the regional viewpoint and give pause to unrestrained majorities in the House of Commons. Yet it would be clear that ultimately, the will of the majority in the House of Commons would prevail.

Other supporters of a suspensive veto power for the Senate have explored variations in the procedures for its application. It has been suggested, for example, that a bill passed by the House of Commons and subsequently rejected by the Senate should require a second adoption by the House of Commons before it could be presented to the Governor General. Detailed procedures relating to timing, to the use of special majorities and to different classes of legislation will require careful attention. The objective must be to structure a balance between the principles of regional representation in a reformed Senate and of majority power in the House of Commons, without producing deadlock or otherwise rendering the parliamentary process too unwieldy. (Vol 3, p. 91).

The one exception to which the Commission refers above is legislation of "special linguistic significance". For such legislation, the Commission recommended that "passage of a law would require the support of both a majority of the Senate and a majority of francophone members." The Senate veto in such matters, it recommended, should "be absolute, not simply suspensive". (p. 91)

A HOUSE DIVIDED

The basic concept recommended by the three reports, of Senate powers less than those of the House of Commons, seems necessary if an elected chamber is to fit into the parliamentary system and if we are to avoid the kind of deadlock that developed in Australia in 1975. The problem is to establish a balance between powers and deadlock that will avoid the danger without producing a Senate that is so weak that it is not effective as the voice and protector of regional interests. As Professor Smiley says:

> No case at all can be made for a weak elected Senate in Canada, a body whose powers can easily be overridden by governments sustained by majorities in the House of Commons. Yet the existence of any other kind of elected second chamber is almost impossible to reconcile with the operative rules of responsible government as Canadians have come to understand them. (p. 35).

While the problem of balance is difficult, it should not be impossible to find a solution through a careful combination of differing powers with respect to defined subject areas. Clearly the government should not be subject to a requirement of responsibility to an elected Senate. Responsibility must be to the House of Commons only. If that principle is to be prevail, a government must also not be subject to financial strangulation by the Senate, as it was in Australia. One solution would be that recommended by the Special Joint Committee: no powers of delay on appropriation bills. Another possibility would be to provide more specifically for a difference in role between the two Houses on taxing and spending. Full control of both could be placed in the House of Commons, with no power of approval, amendment or rejection by the Senate. The Senate's role would be to review taxing and spending measures and to make formal comment and report within a short period of time. To ensure no delay on government financial measures, the period could be as short as five or 10 working days from receipt of a bill. The report could be formally submitted to the Minister of Finance and the Leader of the Opposition in the House of Commons. The right to comment in this way could be politically effective without creating the risk of deadlock between two elected bodies that might, in matters of finance, be dangerous.

EFFECTIVENESS WITHIN THE PARLIAMENTARY SYSTEM

On general legislation, it may be that a suspensive veto, as recommended by the Special Joint Committee and the Macdonald Commission is too limited a power. The alternative to suspension with a House of Commons power to override could be a requirement, when agreement between the two Houses cannot be achieved, for final decision by a simple majority vote in a joint sitting of the House of Commons and the Senate together. In such a joint sitting the less populous provinces and regions would have a greater weight than in the House of Commons. That greater weight would be consistent with the fundamental purpose of the elected Senate with its added representation for the smaller provinces. It would be necessary, of course, to provide that the government should not be considered responsible to any such joint session. The provision in the Constitution would have to be specific that the confidence required for a government is that of the House of Commons alone.

In the case of legislation of linguistic significance, the argument for special treatment is strong and it is a feature of three of the four reports: those of the Special Joint Committee, the Alberta Committee and the Macdonald Commission. Since those reports were written, the Meech Lake Accord has given added reason to have a special provision in the powers of the Senate for any language legislation there might be in future in the federal field. Section 1 of the proposed Constitution Amendment, 1987, would affirm constitutionally the "role of the Parliament of Canada—to preserve the fundamental characteristic of Canada" in relation to our two linguistic communities, the French-speaking "centred in Quebec but also present elsewhere in Canada" and the English-speaking "concentrated outside Quebec but also present in Quebec." The equality affirmed for the constitutional status of the two communities, and the equal obligation of Parliament for preservation of "the fundamental characteristic of Canada" arising from their existence, could appropriately be reflected in a formal equality of process when Parliament acts in matters of linguistic significance. The reformed Senate is clearly the place for that reflection.

On the possible process for a double majority, the report of the Special Joint Committee says:

> To ensure additional protection for the French language and culture, we accept the argument of a number of witnesses

that legislation of linguistic significance should be approved by a double majority in the Senate. Two methods of calculating such a majority were proposed to the Committee. One called for a majority of both francophone and anglophone senators. The other called for an overall majority of all senators that would have to include a majority of the francophone senators.

The second method would, like the first, protect the francophone minority against legislation that they believed threatened them. In addition, it might be easier to get Senate approval of legislation that the francophone minority considered desirable, because the second method would require a larger proportion of anglophone senators— if they were to vote without francophone support—to defeat it than just the simple majority of anglophones required under the first method. Since Senate rejection of such legislation could not be overridden by the Commons, there is an argument for making that rejection by the majority language group more difficult. Because the second method does that, we tend to prefer it.

Such a voting procedure would achieve its purpose only if the Senate veto on these matters were absolute. In other words, a bill or a portion of a bill having linguistic significance could not become law unless it had been passed by a double majority in the Senate. To identify those bills or parts of bills that should be subject to the double majority, it would be necessary to adopt a workable definition and a procedure for resolving disputes.

We propose that, at the time of swearing in, senators would be asked to declare whether they consider themselves francophone for purposes of the double majority. (p. 31).

Questions with regard to other special powers that might or might not be given to an elected Senate were considered in three of the four studies and are reflected briefly in Appendix B. None seems to be either fundamental or necessary for an effective Senate in our parliamentary system. The Macdonald Commission did not recommend any such special powers to ratify appointments to the Supreme Court or to national boards or agencies, to ratify international treaties or otherwise to play a new role in scrutiny of some of the actions of the federal government. It made clear that the Senate "should continue to perform its useful role of applying basic 'sober second thought' to all legislation", to conduct inquiries and to provide the "public airing of issues" as it does today. With such functions continued, the report adds that:

> Commissioners believe that an elected Senate such as we have described would enhance the representative element of the national government by ensuring strong representation from all regions in the caucus of each party and in the Cabinet. We believe that it would strengthen the voice of the smaller provinces and give their people greater confidence that national majorities in government would pay special attention to their interests. Moreover, it would do so by strengthening, rather than weakening, responsible party government. (Vol. 3, p. 91).

The conclusion of the Royal Commission seems right but it has to be read subject to some of the cautions Professor Smiley expresses arising from his study of the operation of the Australian Senate. The Australian experience, he says, "would indicate that the procedures by which members of an elected Senate are nominated and elected are crucial determinants of the ways they will behave". (p. 52). Such procedures cannot all be the subject of constitutional provision but some can be. Consideration will have to be given to the term of office of senators and the handling of elections in the light of their implications on the capacity of the Senate to be effective in its role as a regional forum while still providing for the essential participation of political parties in senatorial elections.

Chapter 8

Some Elements of Structure

The Term of Senators

The Alberta Committee recommended that the terms of senators should be for the life of two provincial legislatures in the province from which a senator comes and that Senate elections, in each province, should coincide with provincial general elections. Such a provision would give a provincial context to the election which would imply, if not require, that the party participation in the Senate elections would be by the provincial party structures. There would also be a context of issues relating to matters of provincial jurisdiction for an election of members to a national legislative chamber. Joining the Senate election to a provincial election would inevitably swamp the federal context in which senators should be chosen. This seems undesirable.

The Special Joint Committee of the Senate and House of Commons recommended a nine-year, non-renewable term for senators with elections separate from the general elections for the House of Commons. The purpose was to increase the independence of senators so that they would be more likely to be free of party constraints in voicing the interests of their regions. While the objective is sound, it seems doubtful whether, on balance, either a non-renewable term or a tenure as long as nine years would be wise. If a fixed term were to be adopted, with the separate elections for senators that would result, a six year renewable term might be preferable.

Both the report of the Canada West Foundation and that of the Macdonald Commission recommended that Senate elections should be a part of federal general elections for the House of Commons. In order to provide a longer term of office for senators than for Members of Parliament, which would increase their independence and stature, the Canada West report recommended that a senator should sit for the life of two parliaments, with half the number of senators from each province being elected at each national general election.

There are disadvantages in both the Special Joint Committee model and that of these two reports. A non-renewable term, as recommended by the Special Joint Committee, would gain independence at the cost of losing accountability to the electors. It also seems dubious whether vigorous participants in public life would wish to seek an office with no future beyond a single term. On the other hand, some Members of Parliament might be attracted by the possibility of a final stage in a political career in which they would be free of party discipline. The role of senior, independent statesman might attract able people whose experience is not now well used. Separate senatorial elections at fixed dates would introduce a rigidity that might not fit well with our flexible parliamentary system. On the other hand, the coincidence of senatorial elections with our general elections, as in the Canada West and Macdonald proposals, would increase the partisan context of the elections and, to that degree, reduce the independence of senators. Indeed, with the inevitable focus of a general election on the selection of a government, it would be extremely difficult for candidates for the Senate to be seen and assessed on any individual basis. They would be swept in or swept out with stronger tides. No design is without its disadvantages.

Constituencies for Proportional Representation

If a distribution of Senate seats among the provinces was established as recommended by the Special Joint Committee, the provinces other than Ontario, Quebec and Prince Edward Island, would elect six senators at each general election. To have effective proportional representation, it would be desirable that each province should be a single constituency electing the six senators. This has its problems with provinces as large as most of ours are but the Australian experience with states of comparable size demonstrates that it is by no means inoperable.

Ontario and Quebec would elect 12 senators at each election. It would be for consideration whether those provinces should each elect their senators from a single constituency or whether it would not be better to divide them into two constituencies, each electing six senators. The latter is probably the most manageable plan.

Prince Edward Island and the Territories would present problems. If half of Prince Edward Island's six senators were elected at each general election there would be very limited "proportional representation", especially with three or more political parties in the field. The best course might be to provide that, in any province or territory with six senators or less, all senators would be elected at every second general election, rather than half at each election.

For the Northwest Territories the Special Joint Committee recommended that there should be four senators and for the Yukon two. These seem reasonable. In the case of the Northwest Territories it might be well for the Constitution to contemplate the possibility of its division into a Territory of Nunavut, as the Inuit favoured in a plebiscite in 1982, and a western Territory, largely Indian, Metis and white. If that were to happen, each new Territory could have two senators, as for the Yukon.

Problems of P.R.: qualifications and alternatives

As has been indicated earlier in this study, Professor Smiley's report on the Australian experience with proportional representation brings out strongly the degree of party control that has come into the electoral process, even though the single-transferable vote system is designed to limit that control. Smiley says:

> The nomination of Senate candidates is made by the State executives of the parties and, to repeat, there are always fewer nominees from each party than the number of seats at stake. The control of the State executives over the electoral process is enormously enhanced by their power to rank their respective party candidates on the ballot and to distribute

the how-to-vote cards to party organizers. In a half-Senate election the candidates ranked first and second in each State are virtually assured of election, the third-ranked candidate's position is always risky. (p. 43)

The consequence of the high degree of control in the hands of party executives is a serious problem for the identity and independence of senators. Smiley adds:

As in Canada, a member of the House of Representatives may build up a local following and retain his political position through effective and visible service to the individuals and communities in his constituency. For a Senator this is not so, the constituency is the State executive of the party. Thus the overtly individualistic and anti-party bias of the electoral system for the Senate has reinforced the dominance of the parties over the electoral process. (p. 45)

While Professor Smiley does not refer to it, a related problem arising from party control and the fact that constituencies are entire states must be that areas of sparse population and small centres will tend to get little representation in the Senate. Certainly there can be no local or regional identification within a state: all senators are from a state as a whole. This system, if adopted for Canada, would probably produce a listing of candidates for election to the Senate with a bias in favour of the large cities—Toronto, Montreal, Vancouver, Winnipeg and comparable centres in other provinces—since those would have the most votes and local identification with them would be of greatest advantage. Solutions of these problems will not be easy.

One possibility might be to qualify the search for proportionality and to increase the emphasis on regional distribution within provinces themselves. A conceivable arrangement might be to have elections take place in constituencies electing three rather than six senators. On this basis, there could be four constituencies in Ontario and Quebec rather than two, and two constituencies in other provinces (except Prince Edward Island) rather than one. The constituency boundaries could be designed to ensure that some representation would come from and be identified with areas other than the metropolitan centres.

Still greater local identification could be achieved by moving to single member constituencies, using the single transferable vote system. (This system of voting in single-member constituencies is also referred to as the "preferential vote" or the "alternative vote" to distinguish it from the STV in multiple-member constituencies.) The alternative vote would ensure that whoever was elected in each constituency had a majority made up of the voters' first, second or lower choices. It would not provide any certainty of proportionality as between parties. With a system of this kind, with half the number of senators being elected at each election, Ontario and Quebec would have 12 constituencies and the other provinces six, except Prince Edward Island which would have three.

Canada had some experience with the use of the alternative vote (AV) in Manitoba in the 1920s, in Alberta in 1935 and in British Columbia in 1952. A study by Andrew Treusch in 1980 for *Parliamentary Government* indicates that the system did not produce results very different from those of the "first-past-the-post system". It did change the results in some seats in Manitoba and British Columbia but Treusch's conclusion is "That experience showed the candidate leading in the first count will almost always win on a subsequent count."

While Canadian experience has been limited, it appears that the use of the alternative vote might prove to be little more than a cumbersome and costly way of providing almost identical results to those that our traditional system of voting produces.

It is clear that the best means of securing an elected Senate that is markedly different in party composition from the House of Commons is by having election in multiple-member constituencies, either three-member or six-member, using the single transferable vote. Some degree of local identification and of regional distribution within a province can be ensured by the use of three-member constituencies. The real question is how best to increase the independence of senators from party control and influence in order to produce a Senate where voice and conduct are truly regional rather than slavishly partisan.

Party control of electoral lists, and thus of electoral results, might be weakened by preventing some of the devices Professor Smiley describes as having developed in Australia.

The listing of candidates on ballots might be required to be alphabetical, rather than by party. Alternatively, if listing by party were permitted, the sequence within each party slate might be required to be alphabetical. Provisions of this kind could eliminate the control by party executives of the advantage that is given by a "top listing" in a party slate. A further protection from strict party control of slates and thus of results might be by providing that no party listing or identification would be permitted unless a party ran at least two more than a full slate of three or six candidates. Block voting would thus be rendered impossible, although not individual selection by the voter of candidates all of one party.

The candidacy of genuinely independent persons, or of representatives of local issues and concerns, seems likely to be rendered more possible through the use of three-member rather than six-member constituencies. Such candidacies are also more likely to be successful if Senate elections do not coincide with general elections. In short, a fixed term for senators could be one of a combination of measures designed to increase senatorial independence while still having party identification and party participation in elections.

While the questions of constituency size, method of voting, listing on ballots and party identification may appear to be tiresome details, it is clear from the Australian experience that any one of them, and certainly all in combination, can have a significant effect on the kind of elected Senate that results. Party participation in the elections is essential if any degree of coherence or predictability is to exist in Senate operation, and without those the process of government at the legislative level would be extremely difficult. On the other hand, the whole objective of genuine regional representation and voice will be defeated if the elected senators react, as now, almost exclusively on the basis of partisan advantage rather than regional view.

Reflection on these problems suggests that the best solution is likely to be found in recognizing the multiplicity of factors that have to be taken into account and in not opting for a deceptive simplicity. Retention of our traditional method of voting in single number constituencies will do little to provide a wider representation of differing regional views. A search for the optimum reflection of proportionality within regions will sacrifice the identification of senators with local areas and with individual voters. Avoidance of party involvement in Senate elections would destroy policy identification and produce a chaotic Senate. Party control of electoral procedures would perpetuate the partisan basis of conduct in the Senate.

Like almost everything in the complex community that is Canada, the most effective result for a reformed Senate within our parliamentary system will have to be a compromise. In this case, however, the compromise will not be about particular regional, linguistic or ethnic interests as our compromises so often are. It will be about the balance we want to achieve in a new Senate for Canada and how best to design the details of electoral process and constitutional structure to produce it.

The "Senate floor" in the House of Commons

The proposed distribution of Senate seats, which would increase the representation of the three Maritime provinces and double that of Newfoundland and of each of the western provinces, raises a question about the "senate floor" on a province's representation in the House of Commons. The report of the Special Joint Committee addressed the question in 1984 in the following paragraph:

> If our proposed distribution is adopted, it would be necessary to amend section 51A of the Constitution Act, 1867, which now provides that a province is always entitled to a number of MPs that is not less than its number of senators. The section should probably be amended to say that the wording should apply only to the number of senators that a province had in 1982. Thus, Prince Edward Island would be guaranteed at least four MPs, but the number would not rise to six when the number of its senators is increased from four to six under our proposed distribution. (p.29)

Since the report of the Special Joint Committee, the situation has been altered by the Representation Act, 1985. That Act dealt with the redistribution of House of Commons seats after each decennial census. It also added to the "senate floor" a "grandfather clause" that provided a new minimum to the number of seats in the House that a province would have in future redistributions. The guarantee now is that no province will have fewer MPs than it has senators, and also no fewer seats than it had in 1976, or during the 33rd Parliament, when the act was passed. These two "floors" guarantee for the future the representation that the four Atlantic provinces now have in the House of Commons. New Brunswick and Prince Edward Island are at their "senate floor" of 10 and 4 seats respectively. Nova Scotia and Newfoundland each have one seat more than their senate allocation—11 and 7 seats respectively. The "grandfather clause" guarantees those for the future.

The question is whether the best course would be to retain these numbers as they now stand for the Atlantic provinces or whether there would be advantages in allowing the distribution of seats for an elected senate to establish new "senate floors". If a new senate floor were adopted, only the four Atlantic provinces would benefit since other provinces are above the 12 or 24 senators they would receive. The new floors would move Nova Scotia, New Brunswick and Newfoundland to 12 seats each from their present 11, 10 and 7 Members of Parliament respectively. Prince Edward Island would move from four to six seats in the House of Commons. For the Atlantic region as a whole the change would be from the present 32 seats in Parliament to 42 as a guaranteed number for the future.

A consideration in favour of adopting the new senate distribution as a floor for membership in the House of Commons is the extremely rapid rate of population growth in Ontario. Quebec and the West will probably have rates of growth sufficient that they will not lose proportionally in too serious a fashion as the House of Commons grows. The Atlantic region, however, will not change in membership as that happens. It will remain either at the present 32 or at the new 42. It would seem not unfair, and probably advantageous for the sense of security of that area, if it were to have the slightly higher guarantee of House of Commons membership that a new senate floor would provide.

Senators and Cabinet Membership

A further question of importance to be addressed in relation to an elected Senate is whether its members should or should not be eligible for appointment to the Cabinet. The Special Joint Committee set out the considerations as it saw them and its own conclusions as follows:

> We considered the question of whether senators should be eligible for membership in the Cabinet. Some members of the Committee attached importance to the government being able to choose senators as ministers in cases where there are not members of the House of Commons of the

government party from a particular province. We feel, however, that appointment of senators to the Cabinet should not be used to overcome the failure of political parties to elect representatives in some provinces. The majority of Committee members also believes that if ministers are drawn from the Senate, cabinet solidarity would prevail over their responsibility as regional representatives. We also consider that the possibility of becoming a minister and the presence of ministers in the Senate would impair the ability of senators to represent effectively the interests of their regions. We conclude therefore that senators should not be eligible for cabinet office or for a position as parliamentary secretary. (p.32)

The Canada West study arrived at the same conclusion. It argued that barring senators from membership in the Cabinet would "institutionalize a formal division of labour that would emphasize the difference between the two chambers". Secondly, it "would imply that a different sort of person would be drawn to each of the two chambers". Its concluding consideration went to the heart of the argument for an elected second chamber:

Third, barring Senators from membership in the cabinet would reduce the extent which Senators were tempted to give a high priority to party political concerns in the hopes of achieving advancement in the form of appointment to the cabinet; it would also reduce the likelihood of regional spokesmen being muzzled or co-opted by the principle of "cabinet solidarity". The imperatives of responsible government mean that a Member of Parliament must represent his party first and his region second; the incentives must be for a Senator to represent his region first and his party second. (p.127)

To meet special situations of need arising from particular election results, the Canada West report has an ingenious suggestion:

In the absence of Commons representation from one or more provinces, a Prime Minister could offer a cabinet position to a Senator. However, the acceptance of a cabinet position should require that he immediately resign his seat in the Senate. A duly elected representative of the region would be serving in the cabinet, and yet the deliberations of the

Senate would remain separate from the direct intervention of Ministers of the Crown. In light of the fact that the Senator had been elected in a recent general election, albeit not in the Commons and albeit to a position that he had been obliged to renounce as the price of his appointment to the cabinet, it would seem justified to extend the "reasonable" length of time during which cabinet members are expected to seek a seat in the Commons until the next general election. (p.128)

The Macdonald Commission differed with the conclusions of the Special Joint Committee and the Canada West study. It argued that one of the benefits of an elected Senate would be precisely the possibility of having there a pool from which Cabinet ministers could be drawn if necessary. The report says:

A Senate elected by proportional representation would usually permit the governing party to constitute a Cabinet that included representatives from all regions because it would contain men and women from all regions capable of assuming Cabinet positions. (Vol. 3, p. 89).

In Australia senators are eligible for appointment to the Cabinet and there are normally a number of ministers drawn from the Senate. However, as Professor Smiley points out in his study, the view of "most recent students of Australian government" is that "the Senate is not and has never been in any genuine sense a State house but rather is a party house." One factor in adding to the party character of the Australian Senate is the fact that it does have a number of Cabinet ministers in it, with their clear commitment to the government of day and to the party discipline that involves. In spite of this, Professor Smiley quotes assessments that the Senate there does make an appreciable difference in favour of the smaller states.

Professor Smiley says:

There is some scattered evidence of an increase in bloc voting by members of small States regardless of party affiliations. In the Question Period, Senators from the small States ask more State-oriented questions than do their colleagues from the larger States. Both in elections for the Senate and House of Representatives and in constitutional referenda on proposals to weaken the Senate, electors in small States show some tendency to regard the Senate as a protector of their interests. Although the evidence in respect to Western Australia, South Australia and Queensland—which in terms of population are over-represented in the Senate—is equivocal, it is quite clear that the Senate is a major protector of the rights of the smallest State, Tasmania, and is regarded as such by Tasmanians. (p.48)

Since the objective of a reformed Senate is to establish a body that will be effective as a forum for the voices and interests especially of the less populous regions of the country, the recommendation of the Special Joint Committee and of the Canada West study that senators should not be eligible for appointment to the Cabinet, presumably with the exception of a government leader in the Senate to direct the handling of the government's program there, deserves serious consideration. However, with the focus of public attention so strongly on government policies and programs and the debate on them in the House of Commons, it seems doubtful whether a prime minister of Canada is likely to depart from the present tradition of choosing his ministers from the House of Commons. There will be very few selected from the Senate except where electoral results make it necessary. The advantage of being able to find a qualified, elected Cabinet member in case of need would seem to out-weigh any possible increase in partisanship in the Senate that would result.

Chapter 9

The Basis for a Renewed Federalism

One would have to be naive to believe that an elected Senate, no matter how it might be devised, would not create new problems for the operation of central government in Canada. The almost certain lack of a party majority in a Senate elected through proportional representation would mean that a government, even with a majority in the House of Commons, would have to give much thought, not only to its legislative program, but also to its policies more generally in order to gain support from senators drawn from parties other than its own. This would be troublesome, yet regional sensitivity of policy and program, rarely a factor of importance in the House of Commons, are a principal objective of an effective second chamber within a federation. There is no way that effective regional balance can be provided in the Senate, especially if it is designed to provide roughly proportional representation of views, that will not impose a new degree of federal discipline on the government of the day. The Royal Commission on the Economic Union and Development Prospects for Canada saw the lack of this balance as a serious defect: what it called "The Institutional Failure of the Centre" in Canada. The report reads:

> Commissioners conclude, therefore, that Canada's national
> institutions of government are not well designed to provide

regional representation or to encompass the regional diversities of Canadian life within the process of national decision making. The principles and practices of representation by population, Cabinet government, party discipline, and majority rule have not encouraged an adequate response to the regionalism of a federal society. In addition, the limitations of regional representation in national institutions have been accentuated, in recent years, by the regional polarization of the party system.

The consequences of this institutional failure have been severe. They have significantly undermined the ability of the central government to act as the national government in either of the senses presented above: the federal government has become less able to articulate and defend a concept that the national interest transcends regional interests; it has become less able to promote reconciliation of competing regional interests in a fair and balanced manner. It has lost some of its legitimacy, thus experiencing reduction of its capacity to act decisively and effectively. (Vol.3,p.80)

The hearings and most of the deliberations of the Commission were completed before the election of 1984 produced, for the first time in many years, a government of Canada with strong support from all regions of the country. The Commission thought it necessary to warn about any impression that the problem was thereby solved. Writing the report after the 1984 election, the Commission cautioned that "persistent regional imbalances in national institutions can ultimately strain the very fabric of Confederation." Its report continues:

Moreover, the less able national institutions are in providing forums for regional reconciliation, the more that role will fall to federal-provincial relations. The less credibly the national government can claim to speak for a region, the more credible become the assertions of provincial premiers that they are the appropriate advocates, not only for matters under provincial jurisdiction, but for matters of federal responsibility, too, and the more citizens will turn to their provincial governments. Indeed, the regional polarization of national politics, is related in complex ways to the growth of provincial government assertiveness and federal-provincial conflict.

> For all these reasons, Commissioners believe that to reform national institutions so that they better represent the whole country in its regional dimensions is a fundamental requirement. The 1984 election of a new government with nation-wide support is encouraging: it shows that even with unchanged political institutions, regional polarization is not inevitable, and that through their own internal processes, political parties can overcome the institutional hurdles. Canadians must recognize, however, that these results were not facilitated by our institutions themselves; indeed, they occurred in spite of our institutional arrangements. It is therefore essential to address the larger institutional issues. (Vol.3,p.81)

It is not surprising that many participants in and students of Canadian politics are sceptical about the importance of Senate reform or about the benefits it might bring for a change in the climate and operation of our political system. Our federal history has been lived with a Senate that has had virtually no significance in the balancing function it should perform either in our public life or in the decisions of governments. The awareness of the nature of that function or of its importance is small except among a few, especially in Western Canada. The possibility that the Canadian Senate, with little federal significance in our entire history as a federation, could be an important factor in resolving one of our most persistent problems thus faces an initial hurdle of disbelief. Several facts should, however, lead even the most sceptical to consider that there may be validity in the proposition.

The four studies examined in this review have all agreed that the essential purpose of a second chamber in a federation is to be a balancing factor to offset disparities among the regions comprising the federal union. They have all agreed that our Senate does not do this and that it cannot do it as long as senators are appointed. They all agree that an elected Senate is needed with a distribution of membership altered to give greater weight to the less populous provinces, especially those of the West and Newfoundland that are so under-represented today. The differences in the reports are on aspects of process and structure: there is complete agreement on the fundamentals. These shared conclusions in four serious enquiries are impressive.

There is also in the four reports agreement on the diagnosis of the problems of our federalism that are characteristic of Canada because of our lack of an effective, federally designed Senate. It is not without significance that these problems appear to be greater in Canada than in comparable democratic federations such as Australia, the United States, West Germany or Switzerland. We are the only federation among the five without a second chamber based on elective principles, effective in powers, and providing a balancing weight of membership for the less populous states making up the federation. This structural failure, and the sense of a grievance long unattended, has served to worsen rather than to ameliorate the tensions that would arise in any case in Canada because of our distances and our regional differences.

Western Canada has insisted for many years that it has been denied the constitutional basis to ensure a fair and reasonable degree of representation and voice in the Parliament of Canada. The results of the elections of 1984 and 1988 have temporarily moderated the problem but they provide neither structure nor confidence for the future. It is not unreasonable that the West should expect action on its long-standing priority for constitutional reform at a time when the basis for a "renewed federalism" is under review.

Nor would it be unreasonable for the provinces of the Atlantic region, in that context, to seek the greater parliamentary weight they will increasingly need with a population that is steadily diminishing as a proportion of our national total. The premiers of both New Brunswick and Newfoundland have in recent months renewed pressure for some change. Premier Wells, at the Interprovincial Conference in Quebec on August 22, 1989, stressed the importance of an elected Senate to "diminish the level of dissension and differences in the country."

It is apparent that the Constitution of Canada, as it stands since 1982, does not provide an acceptable "renewed federalism" as Quebec thought it had been promised in 1980. Removal of the sense of humiliation arising from the acceptance by the rest of the country of a Constitution to which Quebec did not agree is fundamental to the effective operation of Canada.

It was the recognition of those facts that made the Meech Lake Accord possible. However, it is apparent that at least two, and possibly three, provincial governments and legislatures now feel unwilling or unable to provide or to preserve the approvals needed to have the unanimous consent the Accord requires. It is significant that the provinces are all ones that suffer from the lack of structural balance in our Constitution that has long been recognized but ignored. A start on Senate reform may be the only means of alleviating the sense of grievance among Western and Atlantic provinces that is a factor in the public resistance to Meech Lake.

Reopening the Accord in an attempt to amend it would almost certainly be futile if not fatal. With the government of Quebec now under sharp attack for asking so little as the basis of agreement in the Accord, it could not agree to less or to the qualification of critical provisions such as the distinct society clause. Attempting to achieve agreement on a parallel accord that went beyond Senate reform could get into areas so diverse and so controversial that it would deepen rather than lessen difficulties. What is needed at this stage is action in a limited area where there is real hope of resolving the present impasse without introducing new hazards. Senate reform is that area. Reform is desirable in itself: it should have been accomplished many years ago. The considerations have been fully analyzed. The options are not complex: they are ripe for decision. Agreement in that critical area could be the key to agreement on the Meech Lake Accord. It is difficult to see any other solution to the present impasse.

This is not to suggest that agreement on the Accord and on Senate reform would resolve all the constitutional problems of Canada. The vexed problem of aboriginal rights remains without solution after four constitutional conferences. It must still be addressed, but it cannot be successfully addressed until Quebec, with Meech Lake approved, will share in the process. Problems arising from provisions in the Charter of Rights will require attention. There are others. But none of these can be resolved unless the fundamental issue of the position of Quebec within our constitutional framework is settled—and it seems increasingly clear that that may be incapable of resolution unless something is done about the equally fundamental issue of the federal balance between the more and the less populous provinces.

Related to the need to settle these basic questions of structure is the need to stem the growing irritation and misunderstanding that has become apparent in both Quebec and English-speaking Canada in the first half of 1989. In Quebec the connection with the prospective failure of Meech Lake is direct. Public discussion and media comment make it clear that the unwillingness of English-speaking Canada to accept and to implement the Meech Lake Accord is seen as a rejection of modest proposals by Quebec to remove the constitutional injustice of 1981-82. The attack on the "distinct society clause" is seen as a refusal to accept within the Canadian Constitution the undoubted fact that Quebec is different—a fact that is apparent to anyone who makes the briefest of visits to Quebec City, to Montreal or to rural Quebec. The difference is not casual or in the fact of language alone. It is fundamental in the consciousness and thinking of 85 per cent of its people. The fact of difference has been implicitly recognized in specific constitutional provisions long before Confederation and in the British North America Act itself. The bitterness in Quebec over "English Canada's" apparent refusal to recognize this reality was reflected in polls in July of 1989 that showed a higher level of support in Quebec for separation from Canada than at any time since the referendum of 1980. Premier Bourassa's statement that the provincial election of September would provide a new mandate to confront the opponents of the Meech Lake Accord is a reflection of its importance in the province—and of the fact that the only present political alternative is a party that attacks the Accord as providing far too little scope for a distinctive Quebec. Independence is its goal.

In English-speaking Canada, polls in the summer of 1989 showed a growth in readiness to entertain the possibility of the separation of Quebec from Canada. The source of that reaction—or at least the catalyst for it—appears to be, in part, the handling by the government of Quebec of the language issue there in Bill 178 and the use of the "notwithstanding clause" in the Charter of Rights to protect the law from constitutional challenge. The distaste for the Quebec action is not abated by any understanding of the genuine concern of French-speaking Quebec about the future of the French language and culture there. Nor is it offset by any realization that the rights of English-speaking people in Quebec remain, after Bill 178, more complete than those of French-speaking people in any other province and as secure as those in any province except New Brunswick.

What appears to be a Quebec "attack" on the individual rights of the English-speaking in Quebec provides another source of anglophone frustration. It is seen as a direct rejection by Quebec of bilingualism—

exactly what many English-speaking Canadians in Canada generally had thought Quebec wanted and what many of them had come to accept. The number of English-speaking children in French immersion schools and courses in all provinces is a measure, in part, of the efforts of anglophone parents to prepare their children for a bilingual Canada—the bilingualism Quebec is seen now to be rejecting. The frustration and irritation is the more dangerous because it is felt especially among people who had sought to understand the concerns of Quebec and of French-speaking Canadians: the moderate people on whose support national accommodation depends.

There is justice on both sides. On each too there is a profound failure to understand the concerns and the thinking of the other. In the condition of mutual irritation that has grown so alarmingly during recent months there would be great danger either in allowing the Meech Lake Accord to fail or in attempting to open it for revision. There would seem to be equal danger in trying to force or to buy its passage in provinces where opposition is strong. What is needed is one more act of understanding by the people and the governments of both Quebec and the English-speaking provinces that Canada is faced by a serious crisis that has its roots in concerns that are genuine and important on both sides. Accommodation has to be mutual.

Quebec cannot be expected to participate willingly in the Canadian future on the basis of an imposed Constitution. Its history gives cause for confidence in its future conduct under the Accord. Provisions of the Accord afford security against extreme action or alarming interpretations that have been given to some of its clauses.

The West and the Atlantic provinces, for their part, cannot be expected to postpone indefinitely the adjustments in the federal balance that will help to meet their sense of unfairness in the federal structure that was established in 1867 and as it has developed since.

The problems of understanding are not great in relation to what we see in other countries. The capacity of Canadians to find accommodations and to reach constructive agreement is celebrated. A renewed federalism acceptable to Quebec, to the West and to the Atlantic provinces is within our grasp. The interest of Ontario is in helping to promote that accommodation in order to ensure the future stability of the country of which it has been the greatest beneficiary.

The security and the confidence afforded by successful agreement on these fundamental problems would enhance the prospect of resolving the more specific issues that remain.

The critical decisions for Canada's second century of Confederation will almost certainly be taken in the next few years.

Appendix A

The Procedure for Amending the Constitution of Canada

Part V of the Constitution Act, 1982, established for the first time a set of procedures for amending the Constitution of Canada in its entirety. These procedures are set forth in a general procedure (Section 38), a procedure relating to matters of special importance that require the unanimous consent of the provinces (Section 41), a procedure in cases that relate to one or more, but not all provinces (Section 43) and a procedure relating to the executive government of Canada or the Senate and House of Commons (Section 44).

Seven other sections in Part V contain provisions that are procedural or relate to some specific aspect of the amendment process. The final section (Section 49) requires a review of the amendment procedures in a conference of first ministers within 15 years of Part V coming into force—namely, by April, 1997.

The Sections constituting Part V are as follows:

38. (1) An amendment to the Constitution of Canada may be made by proclamation issued by the Governor General under the Great Seal of Canada where so authorized by
    (a) resolutions of the Senate and House of Commons; and

(b)   resolutions of the legislative assemblies of at least two-thirds of the provinces that have, in the aggregate, according to the then latest general census, at least fifty per cent of the population of all the provinces.

(2)   An amendment made under subsection (1) that derogates from the legislative powers, the proprietary rights or any other rights or privileges of the legislature or government of a province shall require a resolution supported by a majority of the members of each of the Senate, the House of Commons and the legislative assemblies required under subsection (1).

(3)   An amendment referred to in subsection (2) shall not have effect in a province the legislative assembly of which has expressed its dissent thereto by resolution supported by a majority of its members prior to the issue of the proclamation to which the amendment relates unless that legislative assembly, subsequently, by resolution supported by a majority of its members, revokes its dissent and authorizes the amendment.

(4)   A resolution of dissent made for the purposes of subsection (3) may be revoked at any time before or after the issue of the proclamation to which it relates.

39.   (1)   A proclamation shall not be issued under subsection(1) before the expiration of one year from the adoption of the resolution initiating the amendment procedure thereunder, unless the legislative assembly of each province has previously adopted a resolution of assent or dissent.

(2)   A proclamation shall not be issued under subsection 38(1) after the expiration of three years from the adoption of the resolution initiating the amendment procedure thereunder.

40.   Where an amendment is made under subsection 38(1) that transfers provincial legislative powers relating to education or

other cultural matters from provincial legislatures to Parliament, Canada shall provide reasonable compensation to any province to which the amendment does not apply.

41. An amendment to the Constitution of Canada in relation to the following matters may be made by proclamation issued by the Governor General under the Great Seal of Canada only where authorized by resolutions of the Senate and House of Commons and of the legislative assembly of each province:

   (a) the office of the Queen, the Governor General and the Lieutenant Governor of a province;
   (b) the right of a province to a number of members in the House of Commons not less than the number of Senators by which the province is entitled to be represented at the time this Part comes into force;
   (c) subject to section 43, the use of the English or the French language;
   (d) the composition of the Supreme Court of Canada; and
   (e) an amendment to this Part.

42. (1) An amendment to the Constitution of Canada in relation to the following matters may be made only in accordance with subsection 38(1):

   (a) the principle of proportionate representation of the provinces in the House of Commons prescribed by the Constitution of Canada;
   (b) the powers of the Senate and the method of selecting Senators;
   (c) the number of members by which a province is entitled to be represented in the Senate and the residence qualifications of Senators;
   (d) subject to paragraph 41(d), the Supreme Court of Canada;
   (e) the extension of existing provinces into the territories; and

      (f)   notwithstanding any other law or practice, the establishment of new provinces.

    (2)   Subsections 38(2) to (4) do not apply in respect of amendments in relation to matters referred to in subsection (1).

43.   An amendment to the Constitution of Canada in relation to any provision that applies to one or more, but not all, provinces including
      (a)   any alteration to boundaries between provinces, and
      (b)   any amendment to any provision that relates to the use of the English or the French language within a province,
may be made by proclamation issued by the Governor General under the Great Seal of Canada only where so authorized by resolutions of the Senate and House of Commons and of the legislative assembly of each province to which the amendment applies.

44.   Subject to sections 41 and 42, Parliament may exclusively make laws amending the Constitution of Canada in relation to the executive government of Canada or the Senate and House of Commons.

45.   Subject to section 41, the legislature of each province may exclusively make laws amending the constitution of the province.

46.   (1)   The procedures for amendment under sections 38, 41, 42 and 43 may be initiated either by the Senate or the House of Commons or by the legislative assembly of a province.

    (2)   A resolution of assent made for the purposes of this Part may be revoked at any time before the issue of a proclamation authorized by it.

47.   (1)   An amendment to the Constitution of Canada made by proclamation under section 38, 41, 42 or 43, may be made without a resolution of the Senate authorizing the issue of

the proclamation if, within one hundred and eighty days after the adoption by the House of Commons of a resolution authorizing its issue, the Senate has not adopted such a resolution and if, at any time after the expiration of that period, the House of Commons again adopts the resolution.

(2) Any period when Parliament is prorogued or dissolved shall not be counted in computing the one hundred and eighty day period referred to in subsection (1).

48. The Queen's Privy Council for Canada shall advise the Governor General to issue a proclamation under this Part forthwith on the adoption of the resolutions required for an amendment made by proclamation under this Part.

49. A constitutional conference composed of the Prime Minister of Canada and the first ministers of the provinces shall be convened by the Prime Minister of Canada within fifteen years after this Part comes into force to review the provisions of this Part.

Appendix B

Recommendations for an Elected Senate

Aspects	Canada West 1981	Joint Committee 1984	Alberta Committee 1985	Macdonald Commission 1985
1. Distribution of seats	*Equality* for provinces—6 to 10 Senators each; Territories 1 or 2 each.	*6 P.E.I.; 24 Ont. & Que.; 12 for other provinces.* N.W.T. and Yukon 2 each.	*Equality* for provinces—6 Senators each; Territories 2 each.	6/24/12 as proposed by Joint Committee. Territories a *total* of 6 (2x3 or 3x2).
2. Method of election	*Single transferable vote.* Elected *at large:* each province a single constituency. Election at same time as *national* general elections.	*First-past-the-post* with *single-member* constituencies. *Separate elections* at fixed dates.	First-past-the-post. Elected *at large:* each province a single constituency. Election at same time as *provincial general elections.*	*Proportional representation*—did not specify what system. Election in *six-member constituencies* at same time as H. of C.
3. Term of office	The life of 2 *parliaments.* 1/2 Senators from each province to be elected at each *national* general election.	*Non-renewable 9 year* term. 1/3 of Senators elected every 3 years.	The life of 2 *provincial* legislatures. 3 Senators to be elected at each *provincial* general election.	*Not clear* whether for life of 1 parliament or 2 parliaments. (Apparently 1 in view of "simultaneous elections of both Houses").
4. Responsibility of the government	To the House of Commons only.	To the House of Commons only. "Senate not be able to overturn a government".		To the House of Commons only (not stated, but implied in suspensive veto, etc.).

Aspects	Canada West 1981	Joint Committee 1984	Alberta Committee 1985	Macdonald Commission 1985
5. Legislative Powers	*Ordinary Legislation:* - Power to amend or reject. - *Over-ride* by H. of C. by an unusual majority.	*Ordinary Legislation:* Suspensive veto only; maximum of *120 sitting days:* 2 periods of 60 days: (1) Senate to act within 60 days of receipt; (2) H. of C. over-ride not less than 60 days after Senate amendment or rejection.	*Ordinary legislation:* - Power to amend or reject. - *Over-ride* by H. of C. by a vote greater in % than the Senate vote.	*Ordinary legislation:* Suspensive veto of 6 months. - no proposal whether "second adoption" by H. of C. should be required. - "detailed procedures" needed re different classes of legislation and use of special majorities.
	Money bills: - No power to initiate. - Power to revise downward or to reject "...be subordinate to the H. of C."	*Money bills:* - No power to introduce. - No power over appropriation bills (suspensive veto = disguised power to overturn government.)	*Money bills:* - No power to initiate. - *No power to veto a supply bill.* - Power to veto a taxation bill with H. of C. over-ride by simple majority.	*Money bills:* No specific proposal.
	Language legislation: No proposal.	*Language legislation:* - *double majority* - *absolute veto*	*Language legislation:* Changes affecting language - *"double majority"* (Majority of Senate and majority of Senators of language affected).	*Language legislation:* - *double majority* - *absolute veto*

Aspects	Canada West 1981	Joint Committee 1984	Alberta Committee 1985	Macdonald Commission 1985
6. Constitutional Amendments	Full veto power (no over-ride by H. of C.).	180 day suspensive veto only		
7. Extraordinary powers of federal governments	Full veto (ratification) of any exercise of unilateral federal powers (no over-ride): - emergency power - declaratory power - reservation - disallowance		Abolish reservation and disallowance.	
8. Appointments	*Not ratify* appointments to the Supreme Court. *Ratify* appointments to designated national boards, agencies and tribunals of special regional significance. *Not ratify* appointment of ambassadors.	Ratify order in council appointments to federal agencies whose decisions "have important regional implications". - within 30 sitting days	*Not ratify* appointments to the Supreme Court (leave this to First Ministers Conferences). *Not ratify* "senior civil service appointments".	
9. Other powers	*Not power to ratify* treaties. Be formally recognized as "an integral part of the formulation of national policy".		Non-military treaties subject to ratification by the Senate.	

82

Aspects	Canada West 1981	Joint Committee 1984	Alberta Committee 1985	Macdonald Commission 1985
10. Procedural	All votes in the Senate to be free votes. Parties in Senate to caucus separately from H. of C. Also caucuses regularly "on a cross-party regional basis".	Senate to elect Speaker after each triennial election. Ministers able to appear in Senate and committees for their legislation. Regional caucuses and political caucuses as now.	*Abolish government/ opposition roles.* Senators sit as *provincial delegations.* 10 provincial chairmen be Senate Executive Council. S.E.C. determine order of business.	Participate in "caucuses of all national parties" to strengthen party government.
11. Relations with House of Commons	(1) Standing Joint Reconciliation Committee to seek "mutually acceptable compromises". (2) If no compromise, over-ride by H. of C. on legislation by *repassage* with an *unusual majority.*		Negotiations with H. of C. be by Speaker of Senate, elected by Senate.	

Aspects	Canada West 1981	Joint Committee 1984	Alberta Committee 1985	Macdonald Commission 1985
12. Eligibility for Office	(a) Senators to be constitutionally *barred from accepting appointment to the Cabinet.* - not an appropriate solution to lack of MPs from a province. - bar would lead Senator "to represent his region first and his party second". (b) Senator appointed to Cabinet to resign Senate seat immediately; be able to remain a Cabinet member until next general election without election to H. of C.; be able to appear before H. of C.to speak on measures relating to his department and to answer questions.	*Not be eligible for cabinet office or as parliamentary secretary.* - not use appointment to overcome failure of political parties to elect representatives from some provinces. - appointment possibility and presence of ministers in Senate would impair ability of Senators to represent regions effectively.	*Not be eligible for cabinet office* - to increase independence of Senators.	*Eligible* for appointment to the Cabinet.

Appendix C

Differences in Electoral Result, 1984 Federal Election

The following tables from Volume 3 of the Report of the Royal Commission on the Economic Union and Development Prospects for Canada provide a useful comparison of the way in which a system of proportional representation could produce results in an elected Senate that would differ greatly from the results in the House of Commons, assuming that our "first past the post" system were retained there.

Table 21-15
1984 General Election Results:
Seats and Popular Vote by Province

Province	Total Seats	Progressive Conservative		Liberal		NDP	
		% Vote	# of Seats	% Vote	# of Seats	% Vote	# of Seats
Newfoundland	7	57.6	4	36.4	3	5.8	--
Nova Scotia	11	50.8	9	33.6	2	15.2	--
New Brunswick	10	53.5	9	31.9	1	14.1	--
P.E.I.	4	52.0	3	41.0	1	6.5	--
Quebec	75	50.2	58	35.4	17	8.8	--
Ontario	95	47.6	67	29.9	14	20.8	13
Manitoba	14	43.2	9	21.8	1	27.2	4
Saskatchewan	14	41.7	9	18.2	--	38.4	5
Alberta	21	68.8	21	12.7	--	14.1	--
British Columbia	28	46.7	19	16.4	1	35.0	8
Yukon/Northwest Territories	3	49.1	3	24.3	--	22.2	--
Total	282	50.0	211	28.0	40	18.8	30

Table 21-4
Projected Distribution of Senate Seats (144) under Proportional Representation as Determined by 1984 Election Results

Province	Progressive Conservative		Liberal		NDP	
	% Vote	# of Seats	% Vote	# of Seats	% Vote	# of Seats
Newfoundland	57.6	7	36.4	4	5.8	1
Nova Scotia	50.8	6	33.6	4	15.2	2
New Brunswick	53.5	6	31.9	4	14.1	2
Prince Edward Island	52.0	3	41.0	3	6.5	0
Quebec	50.2	13	35.4	9	8.8	2
Ontario	47.6	12	29.9	7	20.8	5
Manitoba	43.2	6	21.8	3	27.2	3
Saskatchewan	41.7	5	18.2	2	38.4	5
Alberta	68.8	9	12.7	1	14.1	2
British Columbia	46.7	6	16.4	2	35.0	4
N.W.T. and Yukon*						
Totals	50.0	73	28.0	39	18.8	26

Source: Canada, Office of the Chief Electoral Officer, Thirty-Third General Election 1984: Report of the Chief Electoral Officer (Ottawa: Minister of Supply and Services Canada, 1985).

Note: Table 21-4 shows the provincial distribution of the 144 Senate seats in the 1984 election, assuming the use of proportional representation on a province-wide basis, if voters had expressed the same party preferences for Senate candidates as for House of Commons candidates.

* The distribution of the six seats allocated to the Northwest Territories and Yukon has not been projected because the issues of choosing an electoral system and dividing the Northwest Territories remain to be resolved.

Appendix D

Basic Questions about a Reformed Senate

The discussion in this manuscript rests on propositions that are points of agreement in the four studies it examines. Essentially those propositions, while differing in detail, are that a reformed Senate is important for the successful operation of the Canadian federation; that the reform should have election of senators as its foundation; that there must be a significant weighting of representation in favour of the less populous provinces; and that the powers of the reformed Senate must be significant and effective, while not upsetting the fundamentals of the responsibility of the government of Canada to the House of Commons alone. If those four propositions can be accepted as the basis for undertaking the consideration of the necessary constitutional amendments to establish a new Senate, significant questions will still remain for decision. Among them are the following:

1. **The distribution of seats among the provinces:**

    (i)   Is absolute equality of provincial representation consistent with the realities of Canada, in which 85 per cent of the population whose maternal tongue is French live in one province: Quebec?

    (ii)   If absolute equality is not so consistent, is there any better distribution of Senate seats than the one recommended by the Joint Committee of the Senate and the House of Commons in 1984?

2.   The method of election:

    (i)   Proportional representation? Single transferable vote (alternative vote) in single member constituencies? "First past the post" voting?

    (ii)   If P.R. is preferred (probably the single transferable vote in whole-province or part-province constituencies) how does one have participation by the political parties without delivering too much control of party representation in the Senate to the party executives?

    (iii) If single member constituencies are preferred, how does one get a Senate that is not substantially a replica of the House of Commons?

3.   The term of office:

    (i)   Should it be for a fixed term (six or nine years) or related to the life of the House of Commons or of the legislature of the province from which a senator is elected (probably twice the terms of the chosen body)?

    (ii)   If the term is fixed, Senate elections will occur on a pre-scribed schedule and will be separate from House of Commons elections, which will have the advantage that the choice of senators will not be engulfed in the focus of a general election on the choice of a government. Would that advantage, which would give the Senate more status, more than offset any added rigidity in our political system or any probable reduction in voter participation in separate Senate elections?

    (iii) If the term is flexible (probably the life of two "Houses of Commons") and coincides with general elections, is there any way to reduce the tendency for the choice of senators to be dominated and distorted by voter concentration on the choice of a government?

4. **Powers of the Senate:**

   (a) *General*

   If it is agreed that the Senate should have no constitutional power to pass a vote of confidence or non-confidence in a government with any result on its capacity to continue in office, should the Senate nonetheless be able to debate and to express a view on the program and performance of a government in general?

   (b) *Ordinary legislation*

   (i) Should the Senate have full power to amend or to reject ordinary legislation (possibly with some limit of time for action), or should it have only a suspensive veto (possibly 6 months), subject to override by the House of Commons?

   (ii) If the Senate is given full powers with respect to ordinary legislation, should final decision on any measure in which the views of the two chambers differ be by a joint sitting of the Senate and the House of Commons?

   (c) *Money bills (taxation and appropriation)*

   (i) If the present principles are retained, that taxation and appropriation bills must be introduced in the House of Commons by the government, should it also be made specific (as it is not now) that the Senate should have no power to amend such bills?

   (ii) Should the Senate have the power, within a prescribed period of time, to express a formal view on financial measures, with such view being transmitted to the prime minister or the minister of finance and to the leader of the Opposition in the House of Commons?

Should there be any obligation on the House to debate and vote on such views?

(d) *Language legislation*

    (i) Should legislation of special linguistic significance be subject to a "double majority" in the Senate—a majority of the Senate as a whole and a majority of Senators of the language affected—with power of absolute veto (i.e.—no override by the House of Commons nor by a joint sitting of the two chambers)?

    (ii) In what way should determination be made whether a bill is of "special linguistic significance"?

(e) *Constitutional amendments*

    (i) Should Section 47 of the Constitution Act, 1982, be retained under which a constitutional amendment can be made without a resolution of the Senate after 180 days if the House of Commons again adopts its resolution of amendment?

    (ii) Should any types of amendment be excluded from Section 47 and the Senate be given full powers with respect to them?

(f) *Other powers*

    (i) Should the Senate be given any powers of ratification of any categories of appointment by the government of Canada?

    (ii) Should the Senate be given any constitutional powers or role with respect to treaties or international agreements?

5. Ministers of the Crown:

    (i) Should there be any constitutional prohibition against a senator becoming a minister while still retaining his or her seat in the Senate? If so, should there be exceptions, such as a leader of the government in the Senate, or a situation in which there is no Member of Parliament of the government party from a province to be made a minister?

(ii) If there is a qualified prohibition or no prohibition, should a minister in the Senate have a constitutional right to appear in the House of Commons to deal with questions, legislation or other matters relating to his or her department?

6. The "Senate floor"

If the revised representation in the Senate for a province is greater than at present, should that new representation become a new constitutional minimum ("senate floor") for the representation of the province in the House of Commons?

Bibliography

The Unreformed Senate of Canada, R.A. Mackay: Carleton Library No. 6, revised edition 1963.

Regional Representation: The Canadian Partnership, A task force report prepared by Peter McCormick, Ernest C. Manning and Gordon Gibson. Published by the Canada West Foundation, September, 1981.

Report of the Special Joint Committee of the Senate and of the House of Commons on Senate Reform, January, 1984.

Strengthening Canada, Report of the Alberta Select Committee on Senate Reform, March, 1985.

Report of the Royal Commission on the Economic Union and Development Prospects for Canada, Volume 3 - the Institutional Context, 1985.

An Elected Senate for Canada? Clues from the Australian Experience, Donald Smiley, Institute of Intergovernmental Relations, Queen's University; Institute Discussion Paper 21, 1985.